TRADITION AND CHANGE IN URBAN CHINA

A Critical Hermeneutic Inquiry
of Language, Culture and
Identity in Shanghai

Amy E. Pierovich, Ed.D.

ISBN 10: 0984347593

EAN 13: 9780984347599

TABLE OF CONTENTS

To the memory of my father
Andrew L. Pierovich

ACKNOWLEDGEMENTS

This research would not be possible without the support and generosity of many people, so I wish to thank the following:

my doctoral advisor and dissertation chair, Dr. Ellen Herda, for her teaching and guidance throughout my doctoral journey. I have found Dr. Herda to be a person of exceptional integrity. Over time, one observes that Dr. Herda has congruence between speech and praxis. Dr. Herda exemplifies solicitude and care for the other. She has opened up the world of critical hermeneutic inquiry to me, which lead me to a new way of understanding my purpose and place in the world. Through knowing Dr. Herda, I have appropriated an important message: We are always in relationship with the other, and it is through relationship that we come toward the fullest realization of our humanity.

my dissertation committee members, Dr. Patricia Mitchell and Dr. Betty Taylor, for their guidance and insight into my research. These individuals are committed to a high ethical standard both in teaching and in working with others in the broader community.

my statistics professor, Dr. Mathew Mitchell, and also physicist, Dr. Richard Sears, for shedding light on a difficult subject.

my philosophy professor, Father Denis Collins, for his extraordinary course lectures. Father Collins gave me a deeper understanding of philosophy, phronesis and ethical action. I carry with me fond memories of my discussions with Father Collins.

my former teacher and special friend, Nancy Rubin, who showed me the true meaning of love and compassion.

my husband, Dr. Joseph Leone, for his encouragement to pursue doctoral work. With his support, my studies, research and eventually my dissertation came to fruition. I have appreciated the exchange of ideas between us over these many years.

my step-daughter, Laura Leone, for her dedication and professionalism in editing this text. Laura brought knowledge, expertise, and competency to the assignment.

my sister, Ann Elizabeth Pierovich, for her insight into Shanghai's culture and for her significant contribution to my research library on China and critical hermeneutics.

my son, Victor Sprenkle, for his love and for his ability to tell stories that are truly engaging.

my family and friends for their support and their interest in my research topic.

my research participants and all of the people I met in Shanghai during the spring and summer of 2008. The goodness of the human spirit is alive and well in China.

CHAPTER ONE

THE RESEARCH FOCUS

Introduction

China is experiencing rapid economic growth and is a strong contender in international trade and commerce. Moreover, this country is gaining in military strength. China's tremendous growth and development challenges the United States's position as the primary economic and political leader in the world. With a population of 1,307.6 million people, China's citizens are the country's greatest asset (Hemelryk and Benewick 2008:6). My research site, Shanghai, is unique. Shanghai has been an important trade port city with a high concentration of foreign residents and foreign visitors for most of its history. Hemelryk and Benewick (2008:8) state, "Shanghai is a directly governed municipality, and China's showcase modern city. It is fast turning itself into Asia's telecommunications, logistics and financial hub." This document explores language, culture and identity in present-day urban China viewed through the lens of critical hermeneutic theory. The main focus of this work is an exploration of urban Chinese identity; language and culture together create the substructure that is identity. In terms of theory, this text draws upon the critical hermeneutic concepts of *mimesis*, appropriation, and imagination in particular.

The guiding questions for this research invite the research participant to engage in dialogue and reflection on the following questions: What is significant from China's past that is carried forward into the present? What characterizes Chinese life in modern, urban China? What are the narratives, the stories that seek to be told, of the urban Chinese? China is a nation on the precipice of change. This country is faced with issues such as severe environmental pollution and a growing disparity between wealthy and poor. Furthermore, there is a need for China to address human rights issues and to open up a dialogue on freedom of speech and other associated freedoms sought by Chinese people. China has historical greatness, and the story that is China continues to unfold.

Statement of the Issue

This research seeks to discover and illumine urban Chinese identity. This inquiry draws significantly upon the work of Paul Ricoeur who states that identity includes the self, *ipse*; the other, *idem*; and the dialectic of the two (1992:116). Thus, identity is inclusive of individual identity and also of one's relationship to others in society. Ricoeur submits that we are always in relationship with the other, whether or not we have an awareness of this relationship (1992:116). We hold relationship with the other to such a degree that selfhood cannot be defined without the context of relationship with the other (Ricoeur 1992:116). The Chinese people have an historical awareness of relationship with the other. This tradition emerged out of situations of famine, drought, hardship, and political upheaval. Out of necessity, people needed to rely upon one another to endure and survive during times of chaos and instability. Confucius (551-479 B.C.E.) developed a philosophy of strong hierarchical relationship, wherein well-being emerged from acting in accordance with one's position in society (Higgins 2001:19).

Confucius advocated the virtues of appropriateness, *yi*; ritual, *li*; humanity, *ren*; and filial piety, *xiao* (Higgins 2001:21). Many of these values remain embedded in modern, urban China today.

It is imperative that the United States and other nations move toward an understanding of urban Chinese identity. Clearly, China seeks to assume a greater role in the global arena; and urban China is at the forefront of change. Who are the Chinese? Who are they becoming? And what role will China play in the events that will unfold in the future? To understand urban Chinese identity, we must examine language, praxis, culture, and values. The time has arrived for us to seriously reflect upon the nature of what it means to be urban Chinese in the present day.

Background of the Research Issue

The United States has long held the position of being the economic and political leader in the world. China's growing economic strength changes the balance of power, as China seeks to assume a greater role in world affairs. One problem that impedes China's participation is the ongoing concern about human rights violations. In 1989, the Tiananmen Square demonstrations for freedom of speech and democracy were violently crushed by Communist military forces (Hemelryk and Benewick 2008:29). Ironically, the name Tiananmen means Gate of Heavenly Peace in the Chinese language. In 2006, Amnesty International reported an estimated 1,010 executions in China that included persons who committed nonviolent crimes such as fraud, bigamy, and Internet hacking (Hemelryk and Benewick 2008:28). Another area of significant concern resides in the fact that China has had a pattern of forsaking the environment in favor of rapid economic growth. Hemelryk and Benewick (2008:38) note, "China's consumption of fossil fuels rose by 9.3 percent in 2006, about eight times the US increase of 1.2 percent. China is overtaking the USA as the world's largest carbon emitter." China will need to address these and other pressing issues in order to gain the respect of other nations in the midst of globalization and change. Economic growth alone cannot position China as an emergent world leader.

In this study, early Chinese civilization and the dynastic epoch are discussed; however, this study concentrates on contemporary Chinese history, focusing on the reign of Mao Zedong and the post-Mao era of globalization and China's changing role in global affairs. Mao Zedong proclaimed the establishment of the People's Republic of China on October 1, 1949, yet his full command of Communist Party leadership would last only a decade. Hammond (2004:35) writes, "At a conference of top Party leaders in August 1959, the Defense Minister, Peng Dehuai, criticized Mao." Hammond (2004:35) states that, as a result of this meeting, Mao "had to agree to give up control over the day-to-day management of government affairs." Nonetheless, Mao remained influential following his retreat from daily leadership. Mao continued to hold recognition from the people of China. Furthermore, Mao remained influential in cultural and political affairs in China, albeit from a less visible position. Hammond (2004:34) notes, "From 1949 until his death in 1976, Mao Zedong was the dominant figure in China."

The leadership of Mao was followed by the solidly moderate and pragmatic leadership of Deng Xiaoping from 1978 to 1994 (Hammond 2004:43). Subsequently, in 2003, the comparatively more conservative Hu Jintao assumed leadership of the Communist Party, a leadership characterized by an accommodationist approach (Shambaugh 2008:226). Hu Jintao seeks to listen, increase consultation, and also open up dialogue on pressing issues. However, improved communications must be accompanied by changes in the legal and political realms in order for Hu Jintao to be viewed with legitimacy. Hu is positioned between two generations: an older generation that holds tight to the current hybrid Communist model and a younger generation that would like to introduce further democratic principles into society.

Urban Chinese, especially those adults who are in their twenties and thirties, live in a changing world and they participate in creating the new paradigm. This population holds a past identity that includes the influences of Confucianism, Daoism, and Buddhism. Yet, this population is also influenced by modern history: Communism and the influences of globalization are most apparent in urban China. The past and the present together create present-day identity. Urban residents of present-day China have hopes and dreams for the future in the midst of myriad change and uncertainty.

The concept of change is integral to Chinese philosophy. The Chinese hold the belief that the dragon is the symbol of perpetual change in a chaotic world (Higgins 2001:16). Chinese rulers only hold the Mandate of Heaven, or the right to rule, so long as they act in accordance with the best interests of society as a whole. The succession of dynasties in China was followed by further upheaval and the eventual declaration of Communist rule in 1949. Mao Zedong sought to revolutionize society through an egalitarian ideal strongly influenced by the Soviet model of Communism. Mao brought basic education and thus literacy to people in the rural parts of China. Mao opened medical clinics in remote villages where, previously, there were no health care services. People gravitated towards Mao, as he appeared to represent the will of the people and a return to authentic rule by the Chinese, for the Chinese. Many people in China held the belief that Mao Zedong justly seized power to lead China into a new era of egalitarianism.

Mao's leadership initially seemed to offer hope and promise to the people of China; tragically, Mao's leadership culminated in a dark time for China. The oppressed eventually became the oppressor, and society was turned upside down during the Cultural Revolution. Those who were considered to be intellectuals in China endured severe hardships as scholars were vilified during the Cultural Revolution of 1966 to 1976. Witold Rodzinski (1988:121) writes that the Red Guard youth took part in "tormenting, torturing and beating, often to death, their own teachers." The Cultural Revolution was a time of extreme brutality. Violent persecution was directed at those individuals who were thought to have "bourgeois" tendencies and toward those who "followed the capitalist road" (Fairbank and Goldman 2006:393). People of faith were also persecuted during the Cultural Revolution: Christians, Muslims, Buddhists, and others were targeted for harassment or sent to labor camps. It seems difficult to comprehend how a phenomenon such as the Cultural Revolution could have occurred. Fairbank and Goldman (2006:383) write that the Chinese have no tradition of human rights "because they have been taught that the assertion of human rights (such as due process of law) would be selfish and antisocial and therefore ignoble." Mao's power was not unlike that of an emperor, and, in accordance with Confucian tradition, submission to authority was valued above justice for the individual.

After the Cultural Revolution, new leadership emerged and power shifted to more moderate members of the Communist Party. Gradually, in the post-Mao era, party leaders came to acknowledge that all persons within society have the potential to contribute to the betterment of society, no matter whether one is an agricultural worker, manufacturer, teacher or scientist. In 1989, Deng Xiaoping became the first Chinese leader to travel to the United States when he met with President Jimmy Carter. Deng Xiaoping initiated the "Opening-Up" period, which was largely welcomed by the liberal-thinking Shanghainese and other urbanites. The leadership of Deng Xiaoping allowed for greater educational freedoms and more economic opportunity in China, to include increased trade with foreign nations. However, city dwellers have experienced stronger economic gains than those individuals residing in rural areas, resulting in massive migration from rural areas to urban. The Communist ideal of full equality among citizens remains elusive. China holds many contradictions. The will to survive and the search for the good life appear to reside at the root of Chinese identity.

Today, President Hu Jintao faces the daunting task of reconciling the schism between stated ideals of the Communist Party and the practice of a modified market economy. Perhaps a new narrative of China will come forth to bridge the past and present. Paul Ricoeur (1981:52) writes, "If I can understand vanished worlds, it is because each society has created its own medium of understanding by creating the social and cultural worlds in which it understands itself." This document examines traditional China, modern culture, and the vast influences of globalization in order to move toward a deeper understanding of present-day urban Chinese identity, exemplified in research conversations with selected young, urban Chinese in Shanghai. Critical hermeneutics provides the theoretical framework for this research.

The concept of appropriation submits that we encounter different ways of being-in-the-world (Ricoeur 1998:18). At times, we appropriate or take in that which was previously foreign to us. At other times, we encounter something new and then discard that thought, belief, or way of being. Ricoeur (2004: 107) observes, "The verb 'to appropriate' plays on the possessive and on the verbs signifying to own and to impute to oneself." Appropriation may occur consciously or unconsciously. It is through appropriation that our world becomes enlarged. Shanghai has been and is today a cosmopolitan city. The Shanghainese are continuously encountering foreign ways of thinking and being. The people of urban China take in only that which fits their own identity. Urban Chinese identity is not fixed, but rather it is continuously unfolding and becoming in the present moment.

Ricoeur's concept of threefold *mimesis* holds that there is a past-present, a present-present, and a present-future (1988:4). We are temporal beings. We can experience a present moment;

7

but, at the same time, we can also be in the present-future through our imagination. We can be in the here and now; yet, also be in the past through recollection. Thus, time has fluid, multidimensional qualities. Ricoeur submits that the emphasis is always on the present, as this is the most tangible. Ricoeur (1988:254) writes, "Mortality—not the event of death in public time, but the fact that each of us is destined for our own death—indicates the internal closure of primordial temporality." Ricoeur suggests that we are fragile and we are always in relationship with death. This concept is especially relevant to a study of urban Chinese identity: It is understood in Chinese culture that life is precarious, and conditions may change at any given moment.

Ellen Herda observes that our language reflects our understanding of the world (1999:21). In urban China, people now have words to describe the Internet, cell phone and text message. So, that which was foreign subsequently becomes familiar as new technology influences and changes the cultural milieu. Urban China continues to gain ground in terms of furthering its ability to compete in the international market. Hemelryk and Benewick (2008:48) state, "There is a shift in employment from agriculture to services, such as tourism, hospitality, banking and finance, as China develops a more diverse economy." A new pragmatism has taken root, and this overshadows the puritanical posturing of Mao Zedong Thought that was ubiquitous during the Cultural Revolution. It is apparent that China's present-day economy is a hybrid economy, which incorporates free market enterprise into a socialist economic model. China's governmental leaders vie to compete in the technology and services industries. China is a growing competitor for India, Japan, the United States, and other nations.

Shanghai, posited on the eastern seaboard, plays a key role in China's economy, and this city by the sea has one of the highest population densities in China. Only Shanghai and the capital city of Beijing have a population density of more than 2,000 people per square kilometer; the average in China is 622 people per square kilometer (Hemelryk and Benewick 2005:24). Hemelryk and Benewick observe that "by 2020 China is expected to be a predominantly urban society, with maybe 60 percent of its people living in towns and cities" (2005:26). The urbanization of China signifies a departure from the historic past. China was previously an agricultural-based society. The trend of urbanization has brought increased wealth to city dwellers. However, urbanization has also brought changed culture as more and more people experience stress, anxiety, aloneness, and the erosion of trust. Gains in material wealth have not necessarily been accompanied by an improved quality of life. The Chinese people have long been familiar with the need for survival, and the present-day economic gains do not appear to assuage this sense of living close to death. *Eudemonia*, a sense of enduring happiness, would seem to be elusive in modern, urban China.

Educational Significance

This research contributes to a new understanding of urban Chinese identity. And we must seek to understand the other. In this world of globalization, issues in China readily influence issues in the United States and in other parts of the globe. China is now a major exporter of manufactured goods to the United States and to other nations. Chinese imports influence issues of American health and employment. Erosion of China's forest and pollution in China's rivers may very well affect the delicate balance of the world's ecology. An improved understanding of urban Chinese identity has the potential to contribute to improved diplomatic and business relationships between East and West. Furthermore, understanding Chinese identity can contribute to educational institutions through curriculum development in Asian studies. Thus, this research has implications for furthering understanding within the political sphere and the global economic arena, as well as for expanding upon existing studies in the field of sinology.

It is in our best interest to make an effort to understand urban Chinese identity from an economic view, but there is an ethical imperative as well. The Chinese, like us, suffer, hope and dream of a better world. We inhabit a shared world. Martin Heidegger introduced the concept of *Dasein*, which can be translated as being or existence. A more specific translation of *Dasein* is being-in-the-world (*da*) and being-in-time (*sein*). We are both in time and in a physical locality. Heidegger (1962:206) states, "If we have not heard 'aright,' it is not by accident that we say we have not 'understood.'" Therefore, we must listen to understand. One way to increase our understanding is to engage in conversation. Heidegger (1962:206) reflects, "Listening to… is Dasein's existential way of Being-open as Being-with for Others. Indeed, hearing constitutes the primary and authentic way in which Dasein is open for its ownmost potentiality-for-Being—as in hearing the voice of the friend whom every Dasein carries with it." In the act of listening to the other, we come toward a better understanding of our shared ontology.

Summary

This document analyzes selected urban Chinese narratives and the aim toward the good life in urban China. This critical hermeneutic study has relevance to Sino-global relations and to curriculum development in Asian studies. While there has been extensive research on China, there remains an element of mystery and enigma about China. What are the historical influences on the urban Chinese? What are their values today? How do we come to understand the multifaceted nature of urban Chinese identity? And how do we describe the unfolding of who the Chinese seek to become, in light of divergent beliefs and differences of opinion within society? There are those who mourn the loss of pure Maoism in Communist China. There are others who speak out for democratic reform. Existing literature tells us that urban Chinese identity is complex and that it is not readily understood. This research attempts to contribute to furthering an understanding of urban Chinese identity. One aspect of Chinese identity that is difficult to grasp is that the Chinese manner of communication is subtle and indirect. We must seek to understand that which is said, that which is implied, and that which remains unarticulated.

It is necessary to listen to the narratives of the urban Chinese, and to recognize the historical framework of China, to come towards an understanding of present-day urban Chinese culture and identity. Paul Ricoeur (1992:352) states that we must recognize the self "as being enjoined to *live well with and for others in just institutions and to esteem oneself as the bearer of this wish.*" Thus, in order to come toward an understanding of the good life, it is necessary to explore self, the other, and relationship with the other. Urban Chinese identity is explored through critical hermeneutic inquiry. Research conversations with people in Shanghai, China, are viewed through the hermeneutic concepts of *mimesis*, appropriation, and imagination. *Mimesis* is a concept of temporality, to be described in detail in Chapter Four. The themes that emerge from the conversational text shed light on who the Chinese are and who they are becoming. Urban dwellers are often those who are positioned on the edge of change and who can point toward that which is to come. In the Chinese language, the characters for China are *zhong* and *guo*, or "Middle Kingdom." Historically, the Chinese saw themselves as being posited at the center of the earth. To be sure, the Chinese seek to regain a central position in the world today. Chapter One has discussed the Research Focus. Chapter Two presents the Background of Shanghai. Chapter Three contains the Review of Literature. Chapter Four reviews the Research Process in detail. Chapter Five addresses Data Presentation and Preliminary Analysis. Chapter Six offers Secondary Analysis, and, finally, Chapter Seven presents Summary and Conclusions.

CHAPTER TWO

BACKGROUND OF SHANGHAI

Introduction

The site for my critical hermeneutic research on urban Chinese identity is Shanghai, China. The two characters in Chinese for the name of the city are *shang* and *hai*, which literally mean "ascend" and "sea" (Yuan and Church 2000:50, 105). The name Shanghai has been poetically translated as "to the upper reaches of the sea." Understanding the Chinese language offers great insight into Chinese thought. Translations of Chinese into other languages can, quite naturally, lose the full meaning of the word or concept; of course, this phenomenon of the approximation of meaning is true for the translation of other languages as well. The naming of things is extremely important in Chinese culture. Confucius urged *cheng ming* or "the attunement of names" (Higgins 2001:22). Confucius believed that "words should correspond to realities" (Higgins 2001:22). This philosopher viewed language as "a medium for interpersonal relationships," and he thought that, "to function well, language must be attuned" (Higgins 2001:22).

In modern times, the Communist government decided to name the city of Shanghai the "City of Harmony" for the World Exposition that took place in Shanghai in 2010 (Hemelryk and

Benewick 2008:9). The word "harmony" has great significance to the Chinese way of thinking. In traditional Chinese culture, it was believed that individual desires should be subsumed to the greater good of society. This mode of thought continues on in the present day, although this belief is challenged to some extent by the one-child policy cultural shift. The Shanghainese youth are predominantly from one-child families and this quite naturally changes the dynamic of family relations. The one-child son or daughter no longer has relationships of sharing with siblings, which, in turn, influences the individual's relationship with society. In order to provide a brief overview, the following topics are addressed: Population and People, History, Economic Development, Language, and Education.

The Story of Shanghai

Population and People

Shanghai is a busy port city with a population of 18.2 million; there are an additional 4.3 million migrants who inhabit the city without legal status (Hemelryk and Benewick 2008:9). The city of Shanghai hosted the World Exposition in 2010. Shanghai, an international city on the forefront of globalization, was well suited to host this event. As stated previously, the governmental nomenclature for Shanghai is the "City of Harmony." A striving toward harmony is readily apparent in modern Shanghai, with generally polite citizens and relatively clean parks for a city of this magnitude. There would seem to be a spirit of cooperation as one navigates crowded streets and public transportation. One observes that the Shanghainese in turn accede to the other. Yet, in their everyday lives, the Shanghainese struggle with issues such as fierce competition for jobs, expensive housing, pollution, a lack of private space, and the sense of alienation that can sometimes accompany urban life. The narratives of those who inhabit urban China can best describe the reality of that world. Richard Kearney (2002:4) states, "Every life is in search of a narrative. We all seek…to introduce some kind of concord into the everyday discord and dispersal we find about us. We may, therefore, agree with the poet who described narrative as a stay against confusion." The act of emplotment gathers together seemingly discordant events into a coherent story. In reference to Aristotle, Paul Ricoeur (1988:190) writes, "A good plot must be probable or necessary." Thus, the good plot makes sense. It reveals the meaning that lies within the scattered events that have occurred over time. We each seek to tell our story, and there is meaning to be found within each lived experience. Kearney (2002:4) submits, "Narrative provides us with one of our most viable forms of *identity*—individual and communal." In this statement, Kearney echoes Ricoeur's hypothesis: Identity includes the self, the other, and the constant relationship of the two. As it is true for all of humankind, the Shanghainese inhabit a shared world.

History

Kenneth Hammond (2004: 5) writes, "Modern *homo sapiens* remains appear in China about 40,000 years ago." Archeological records reveal that the earliest people to call themselves Chinese lived on the North China Plain. "States" gradually emerged, which included "numerous tribal groups who defined themselves in contrast to the surrounding 'barbarians'" (Hammond 2004:5). Chinese civilization slowly expanded, and neighboring peoples were usually either displaced or assimilated into the majority group. Some non-Han peoples continued to live in proximity to the much larger Chinese population, and they retained distinctive cultures. Hammond (2004:5) writes, "The use of stone tools gradually became more advanced. Circa 10,000 B.C.E., there was a critical development for the emergence of

Chinese civilization: the domestication of rice occurred, which lead 'to the rise of more complex cultures.'" Distinctive pottery styles were seen between 7,000 and 6,000 B.C.E. In addition, new social elites developed, which were often associated with shamanic cults. Hammond (2004:5) observes, "Somewhere around 5,000 years ago, people in both north China and in Sichuan began to mine and smelt copper, tin, and other metals and to cast bronze objects." Hammond (2004:6) notes that these Neolithic cultures "were characterized by the use of pottery and the creation of settled farming communities." It is evident that the developments that took place during this early period in China's history set the stage for the civilization that would emerge during the dynastic period in China.

The beginning of the dynastic period commences with the reign of the Xia dynasty in 2100 B.C.E. in the Yellow River Valley (Hammond 2004:7). The dynastic period of Chinese history continued on into the twentieth century. This period did not come to a close until the last Qing emperor abdicated the throne on February 12, 1912 (Hammond 2004:45). The dynastic period of China's history was characterized by the rule of one clan or family that had absolute power to rule and govern society. There were particular developments during each dynasty. One notable development was the art of writing. Edward Shaughnessy (2000:190) writes, "The Chinese considered calligraphy to be one of the higher art forms. When it first appeared in China, writing was thought to be imbued with magical power. The earliest forms...were written or carved on turtle shells, ox bones, and bronze vessels ca. 1200 B.C.E." Shaughnessy (2000:190) states: In Chinese mythology, "the creator of the writing system was Cang Jie, who invented ideograms by observing natural phenomena such as prints left by bird claws and animal paws, shadows cast by trees, and heavenly constellations." The Chinese language is rich in symbol, metaphor and nuance, and in its ability to convey multiple meanings within one word or thought. For example, the word "capitalism" in Chinese includes four characters, "capital, property, rank, grade," that together mean capitalism (Gao 2000:67). It is apparent that the Chinese meaning of capitalism is different than the English language meaning of capitalism.

Other significant artistic developments during the dynastic period include Chinese landscape painting; Chinese theater called *canjunxi* or "adjutant play"; *Shi Jing*, (*The Classic of Poetry*); and traditional Chinese music (Shaughnessy 2000:204-206). Shaughnessy (2000:206) states, "The most common instruments included bronze bells, stone chimes, bamboo or bone flutes, clay ocarinas, drums made of skin, mouth-organs... and zithers and lutes." There were also technological advances during the dynastic period. In particular, there were advances in farming, architecture, medicine, military technology, transportation and communication. The Chinese had an impressive understanding of astronomy. Shaughnessy (2000:126) notes that in premodern China, "there was no categorical distinction between astronomy and astrology."

Chinese philosophy includes the beliefs of Daoism, Confucianism, and Buddhism. Kathleen Higgins (2001:16) states, "Dao is a term for the world as a flowing whole." The world is seen as a place of constant change, which is represented in the symbols of *yin* and *yang*. Higgins (2001:17) notes that *yin* and *yang* "originally referred to the sunny side and the shady side, which are relative concepts." Opposites change into each other. Higgins (2001:16) observes, "Chinese thinkers seek to discover the Dao (or 'Way') of nature and the patterns of natural change." In contrast, Confucius believed that the ills of society would be best addressed through highly structured political and educational systems. Higgins (2001:18) writes, "Confucius urged the cultivation and revitalization of traditional ritual practices as the means of forging and reinforcing benevolence and a spirit of cooperation." Confucius's revolutionary idea was that nobility is a function of merit and cultivation, and not birth (Higgins 2001:18). It would seem likely that, in the modern era, Mao

Zedong was influenced by this Confucian thread in Chinese history, restating the claim that neither status nor rightful rule should be inherited. While Daoism and Confucianism emerged during the sixth century B.C.E., Buddhism did not arrive in China until the first century C.E. Many Chinese people readily appropriated Buddhist thought, as it fit well with the Chinese understanding of the nature of being-in-the-world. Higgins (2001:34) observes that Chinese Buddhism "came to see the universe as the manifestation of an Absolute Mind, or the Buddha-nature." Higgins (2001:11) states that in Chinese Buddhism, *samsara*, "the chain of causation that extends through the cycle of rebirth," is *nirvana*. The world of the Buddha is this world. Higgins (2001:34) writes, "All things are already 'perfectly enlightened.' We only need to recognize this." Both urban and rural China have been influenced by Daoism, Confucianism, and Buddhism, and these currents run deep in Chinese thought today.

And so the question arises: How did modern China depart from the long-entrenched tradition of dynastic rule? Perhaps the Mandate of Heaven was lost. Mao Zedong and his followers likely thought that the power to govern should rightfully be seized, as the Qing rulers had failed to protect their people. The British were marketing opium in China in the early 1800s, and this threatened to erode traditional Chinese values and ways of life. Hammond (2004:14) states, "The Opium War of 1839 to1842 ushered in a new age in China's relations with the outside world." Hammond (2004:14) recollects: In 1842, "the Qing were forced to sign the humiliating Treaty of Nanjing… The treaty required the Chinese to open ports along the coast to British and other foreign traders." European nations vied for Chinese territory and attempted to seize control of Chinese goods. The Boxer Rebellion of 1899 was an effort to rid China of foreign domination (Hammond 2001:20). China also suffered under foreign conquest during the Japanese invasion and ensuing war of 1937 to 1945 (Hammond 2004:42). China, once great and sovereign, seemed to be losing the battle for autonomy and self-rule. The situation was ripe for dramatic change, and thus entered Mao Zedong and the Communist Party. Mao and his followers believed that he was reclaiming China for the Chinese with the establishment of the People's Republic of China in 1949. And the idea of change was not so foreign to the Chinese, who believed that the shady side would eventually return to the sunny side.

Shanghai was one of the port cities that had been forced to comply with the Treaty of Nanjing. Posited on the central eastern seaboard, Shanghai had long held the position of being an important trade city in China. Shaughnessy (2005:75) states, in the mid-1800s, "Shanghai, with its superior access to China's markets and resources, quickly emerged as the country's commercial and industrial capital." Shaughnessy (2005:75) also notes, by the year 1900, "Shanghai was generating two-thirds of China's foreign trade and nearly half of its modern factory output." Shanghai culture had long been a place where arts, fashion, and music flourished. During the pre-Mao era, Shanghai was often called "Queen of the Orient." Many Shanghainese were well educated and spoke foreign languages, having come into contact with foreigners through international trade and commerce. It should be noted that not all Shanghainese wanted to oust foreigners from Chinese lands. Prior to the establishment of the Communist government in 1949, the Shanghainese sometimes appropriated foreign ways and dressed in Western garb. However, all cities, especially Shanghai, fell out of favor during the reign of Mao Zedong.

Mao believed that it was the rural worker, the peasant, who should be esteemed in the People's Republic of China. Mao believed that the country would progress through land reform and collectivization. Hammond (2004:34) writes, in 1956, Mao urged "an accelerated program, which soon led to the creation of the People's Communes, large-scale units of collective farming." There was an effort to encourage production and growth in urban China during the Great Leap Forward of 1958 and 1959; however, these efforts to "mobilize peasant labor" in industrial growth failed dramatically, and there were widespread food shortages during these years (Hammond 2004:34). During the Cultural Revolution of 1966 to 1976, the modern thinking Shanghainese suffered greatly. The educated were labeled traitors, and those who had actively engaged in commerce and trade with foreigners were deemed "Capitalist Roaders." Many so-called intellectuals and entrepreneurs were sent to reeducation, hard-labor camps in the countryside during this decade.

It was not until the leadership of Deng Xiaoping emerged in 1978 that China began to regain economic stability, and the climate of fear that was so prevalent under Mao diminished. Hammond (2004:38) states, the 1980s "was a great period of development, as China became more engaged with the global economy." There were significant market reforms: Special Economic Zones were set up to encourage investment, and private enterprises grew, which contributed to economic growth (Hammond 2004:38). The benefits of economic growth are readily apparent in Shanghai, a city of abundant parks, museums, and public libraries. The city of Shanghai once again provides a base for numerous international companies. The policy changes that have occurred in China over the past three decades have allowed present-day Shanghai to return to her identity as a city that is artistic, international, and entrepreneurial in nature.

Economic Development

In 2008, the gross domestic product (GDP) in Shanghai was 57,310 yuan per person (Hemelryk and Benewick 2008:9). It is readily apparent that the Shanghainese are an industrious people. Shanghai citizens earn an estimated monthly wage of 750 yuan, working primarily in the services and industry sectors of the economy (Hemelryk and Benewick 2008:9). However, there would seem to be a tension in modern Shanghai life. The living area per person is only 16 square meters (Hemelryk and Benewick 2008:9). Moreover, many people have been displaced by the Chinese government's relocation and development policies. Hemelryk and Benewick (2008:9) write: "From 1998 to 2002, 15 square kilometers of Shanghai's old neighbourhoods were demolished." Hemelryk and Benewick (2008:9) further state, in the year 2006 alone, "70,000 people were relocated to make way for new developments."

Shanghai, along with Shenzhen and Guangzhou, is a Special Economic Zone with greater free market enterprise (Gaetano and Jacka 2004:19). The entrepreneurial Shanghainese must shift and adapt in an uncertain world. Contemporary Shanghai appears to be rife with change and instability. And yet, the city still draws more to her, as people seek out greater economic and educational opportunities in search of the good life. Chen, Clark, Gottschang, and Jeffery (2001:145) suggest, "There is no static divide between the urban and the rural...Like the Chinese symbol for yin and yang, the urban can be found in the rural and rural resides in the urban." In modern times, there is greater movement of peoples between rural and urban areas. Urban Shanghai culture and rural China share a common history, and the boundaries of rural and urban overlap as people increasingly come into contact with the other. However, the relationship of urban citizens and migrant peoples can be strained. The people who migrate from the countryside to the city without a legal permit are sometimes derogatorily referred to as the "floating population." The newcomers do not have the same rights to employment, education and housing. People who have legal status in urban China may be resentful of the resources taken by immigrants, and the relationship between rural and urban populations can be one of tension and mistrust, which further contributes to the climate of alienation in urban China.

Language

The Shanghai dialect is distinct and unique. It is not readily understood by Mandarin speakers who are not familiar with this dialect. In addition to the Shanghai dialect, various other dialects are found in Shanghai, since migrant workers come to this port city from other parts of China in search of employment. The people of Shanghai are generally well educated, and the vast majority of Shanghainese speak both the Shanghai dialect and Mandarin. Mobo C. F. Gao (2000:16) writes, "The word 'Mandarin' itself originally meant 'official of the imperial court' in traditional China. Therefore, the original meaning of 'Mandarin Chinese' was 'language of the officials.'" Since the establishment of the People's Republic of China, Mandarin has been designated as the official language of China. Gao (2000:16) notes that people in present-day China refer to Mandarin as "*Putonghua*, literally meaning 'the common language.'" Mandarin is no longer for officials only; today, Mandarin is the language of the people. In Shanghai, young people are also encouraged to learn foreign languages, English in particular. In Shanghai schools, the English language is generally introduced as a course of study at the first grade level. Speaking English as a second language is highly valued by the Shanghainese.

Education

Shanghai today has a total of 60 universities that offer studies in various disciplines (Hemelryk and Benewick 2008:9). Historically, Shanghai has long had the tradition of being a place of learning, and modern Shanghai reflects this tradition. As in other parts of the country, most institutions of higher learning in Shanghai were closed during the Cultural Revolution. Julia Kwong (1988:5) writes, "Mao emphasized the power of ideology in transforming the individual." Kwong (1988:29) notes that university campuses were instead used "to hold criticism meetings, plan strategies, write wall posters, and promote the revolution." Traditional education was replaced by violence and the dogmatism of Mao Zedong Thought during the epoch of the Cultural Revolution. From 1966 to 1976, Mao's own writings were widely distributed. At the same time, foreign texts were banned and burned. There is a notable precedent to this violence: In 214 B.C.E., Qinshihuangdi, meaning the "First Emperor of the Qin," ordered the "burning of books and burying of scholars" to eliminate from society what he thought were unorthodox ideas (Hammond 2004:22). Modern Shanghai endured the hardships of the Cultural Revolution and is, once again, a place of great learning and artistic endeavor.

Summary

Shanghai would seem to hold a core identity of being open to new ideas, on the forefront of change, and constantly in flux. It is a place of growth and entrepreneurship. This city is significant to China's increasing role in the phenomenon we call globalization, which is reflected in the modified market economy and in the current movement to open up to foreign concepts and foreign ways. Shanghai identity includes its historic past and its present-day ways of being. The city today faces challenges such as pollution, rising crime rate, unemployment, lack of adequate housing, displacement, migration of new peoples, and the clashes that sometimes ensue when the "floating people" compete with those who have legal rights to work and live in Shanghai (Newman 2005:47). There appears to be a growing disparity between the wealthy and the poor in urban China. In summary, Shanghai appears to be a place of opportunity, but also a place of tension and struggle. It is through the narratives of urban Chinese that we can come toward a deeper understanding of their unique identity.

CHAPTER THREE

REVIEW OF LITERATURE

Introduction

This review of literature explores works that are relevant to understanding urban Chinese identity. Chapter Three's review includes the texts of early anthropologists and significant critical hermeneutic authors. It also includes a review of literature that addresses Chinese language, history, culture, and philosophy. The early anthropological authors will be discussed again in Chapter Four, The Research Process, but from a different perspective. The three main research categories directing this exploration are: 1) *Mimesis*, 2) Appropriation, and 3) Imagination. *Mimesis* may be generally defined as temporality. Appropriation signifies the act of taking in something as one's own. Imagination is the realm of thought of a future not yet made manifest. Through this investigation, a deeper understanding of tradition and change in urban Chinese identity is revealed. This document seeks to understand who the Chinese were, who they are now, and who they are becoming. Hemelryk and Benewick (2008:14) state, "Over one-fifth of people in the world—1.3 billion—live in China." China is an emerging power on the world stage. It is imperative that the United States and other nations seek to understand the people of China. In this manner, we can engage in meaningful dialogue with those who seem different, but who share the ontological condition of seeking the good life in a fragile and precarious world.

Anthropological Research

The work of various early anthropologists is relevant to an exploration of urban Chinese identity. Victor Turner's text, *From Ritual to Theatre*, discusses praxis as play and ritual. Turner (1982:78) states, "Cultural performances may be viewed as 'dialectical dancing partners'...of the perennial social drama, to which they give meaning appropriate to the specificities of time, place, and culture." Thus, according to Turner, human action and cultural meaning are bound within time, place and culture. Turner highlights the importance of context. In order to understand urban Chinese identity, it is necessary to examine China's history, geography, and cultural developments, both past and present. Turner also observes the importance of ritual in society. The practice of ancestor worship in China dates back to the reign of the Xia dynasty in 2100 B.C.E. (Hammond 2004:7). Ancestor worship continues on in present-day China. Turner's work contributes, in particular, to an understanding of the research themes of *mimesis* and imagination.

In her work, *Patterns of Culture*, Ruth Benedict (1934:44) writes, "The history of culture is in considerable degree a history of their nature and fates and associations." Benedict provides a framework through which one can view a culture and a people. For Benedict, culture reflects the whole of a people's history, to include the particular and sometimes peculiar events and associations that make up identity. Kathleen Higgins (2001:17) states, according to Chinese thought, "the human being, like every other thing in the world, is made of *qi*, configured energy." Furthermore, the Chinese view holds that everything is interdependent (Higgins 2001:16). Benedict submits that these kinds of specific beliefs are what create identity. Benedict's work emphasizes the importance of recognizing patterns that endure over time. In China today, there remains a tacit understanding that *qi* is energy, and that all things and people have relationship. Benedict's work is relevant to the research theme of *mimesis* and also to the research category of appropriation. If we examine that which is kept, and that which is discarded over time, then we see that which has been appropriated.

Clifford Geertz's (1983:233) text, *Local Knowledge*, addresses the "interpretive turn," which is "the conceiving of human behavior and the products of human behavior as 'saying something of something.'" Geertz would seem to be aware that action punctuates time, and in language, we seek to describe our world. In his work, *The Interpretation of Cultures*, Geertz examines the meaning of ritual, symbol, ideology, and the political arena. This work provides a lens through which one can examine the social and political phenomena of China. In particular, Geertz's exploration of the political sphere would seem to be relevant to China and to the Cultural Revolution in particular. Geertz (1973:319) submits that "there is...no simple progression from 'traditional' to 'modern,' but a twisting, spasmodic, unmethodical movement which turns as often toward repossessing the emotions of the past as disowning them." Geertz illumines the way the past is intertwined with the present and that the development of culture is not merely a linear continuum. The concept of the Mandate of Heaven, developed during the Zhou Conquest of 1045 B.C.E., was likely a seed in the mind of Mao Zedong when he seized power and declared the People's Republic of China in 1949 (Hammond 2004:11). The burning of books and burying of scholars, which took place in 214 B.C.E., is not unlike the violence that took place during the Cultural Revolution of 1966 to 1976. We can see that Geertz brings to light an important point: history is often cyclical and patterns may submerge and reappear over time. The work of Geertz is particularly relevant to the research categories of *mimesis* and imagination.

Finally, the work of Claude Levi-Strauss is applicable to understanding urban Chinese identity. In *Myth and Meaning*, Levi-Strauss (1978:41) proposes, "Each type of story belongs to a given group, a given family, a given lineage, or to a given clan, and is trying to explain its fate, which can be a successful one or a disastrous one." The story that is China would seem to vacillate between victory and disaster. The history of China is not a stagnant one, rather the story of China is one of flux and change. China has moved from greatness to the depths of sorrow and despair, and back again. And so the story contains both triumph and sorrow. Perhaps the pendulum will now swing toward greatness, as China is perched on the edge of becoming a major contender in the global arena within the phenomenon we term globalization. Although Levi-Strauss is a structuralist, and not a critical hermeneuticist, his work is relevant to the research themes of *mimesis*, imagination, and appropriation.

Levi-Strauss observes that a people are trying to make sense of their own story, and thus come toward an understanding of their purpose in life. In the storytelling, people gather together discordant events into concordance. In other words, people endeavor to emplot their story and find meaning. In modern, urban China, there would seem to be a crisis of identity. How do I reconcile who I am with who I am supposed to be? And how do I heal from the past without a new narrative to make sense of that past? The government has the difficult task of reconciling Communist ideals with the reality of a modified market economy. The gap between the "haves" and "have nots" grows wider. Furthermore, there has been minimal public dialogue of the trauma that took place during the Cultural Revolution. This history, fixed in time, cannot be ignored. The Chinese government must create a new narrative that reflects the truth of past events and present-day realities. Otherwise, this schism between stated purpose and reality cannot be reconciled. It may be that, without a new narrative, there can be no peace in the Middle Kingdom.

Critical Hermeneutic Research

This section discusses the theory of critical hermeneutic writers that have been used in my research. These authors are also discussed in terms of the research process in Chapter Four. Ricoeur's work addresses all three of the research categories, which are *mimesis*, appropriation, and imagination. In particular, the following texts will be referenced: *Oneself as Another*; *Hermeneutics and the Human Sciences*; *Memory, History, Forgetting*; and *Time and Narrative* (Volumes I, II, and III). In *Oneself as Another*, Ricoeur defines identity as inclusive of selfhood, *ipse*; sameness, *idem*; and the dialectic of the two (1992:116). Ricoeur's concept of *ipse-idem* is critical to understanding a relational concept of identity. In China, an awareness of relationship with the other dates back to the beginning of the dynastic era, and perhaps even further back in time. Confucius further brought forth this concept of relationship to the other in Chinese society. Kathleen Higgins (2001:18) writes: Confucius believed that "a society, like a family, should be one in which every member is responsive to, and responsible for, others." A core belief in Chinese culture is that a person always lives in relationship to others rather than separate from or indifferent to the other.

Hermeneutics and the Human Sciences provides a context for understanding our ontological and temporal condition. Ricoeur (1981:294) writes, "We belong to history before telling stories or writing history." We enter the world at a particular place, into a unique culture, at a specific point in time. We cannot separate our identity from our history. The people of urban China who are in their twenties and thirties are acutely aware of the tremendous economic growth of recent decades. At the same time, there would seem to be an underlying awareness of events past. We learn from our elders. And the faces of urban Chinese elders can tell a tale even if no words are spoken. There is a subtle awareness that there have been hardships and sufferings—some events so horrific that people do not speak of them. The relative wealth of modern times stands in strong contrast to the extreme suffering and deprivation that occurred during the Cultural Revolution. Thus, the current hold on wealth may seem tenuous for those who have in fact benefitted from the free market economy. This dramatic shift from abject poverty to apparent wealth within a relatively short time span may create anxiety for many within contemporary urban China.

In *Memory, History, Forgetting*, Ricoeur reflects upon what is recollected, what happened in time, and what is forgotten; that which we keep from time is appropriated. Ricoeur also addresses how we come toward identity within this context. Ricoeur (2004:129) submits that the naming of people and things has power:

> Each of us bears a name that we have not given to ourselves, but have received from another: in our culture, this is a patronym that situates me along a line of filiation, and a given name that distinguishes me from my siblings. This word of the other, placed upon an entire life, at the price of the difficulties and the conflicts we are familiar with, confers a linguistic support, a decidedly self-referential turn, to all the operations of personal appropriation gravitating around the mnemonic nucleus.

In traditional China, a daughter would sometimes be named *Zhao Di*, or "beckoning for a little brother" (Gao 2000:47). And so, one's identity was to be she who brings forth another, namely, a male child. The person given the name *Zhao Di* likely questioned her own value and may have struggled to determine her true identity. Mobo C. F. Gao (2000:47) observes that, "during the time when Maoism dominated China, personal names…became very politicized." Babies were given names such as *Tu Gai*, meaning "land reform"; *Yuan Chao*, "aid Korea"; and *Yong Hong*, "forever red." With each of these names, individual identity was to be subservient to national goals. The name reflected communist goals or ideals; thus, as with *Zhao Di*, it would be difficult to realize self-worth and come toward an *ipse*-identity. The original given name surely leaves an imprint even if, later in time, one is able to define oneself differently.

Ricoeur's work in *Time and Narrative* invites us to reflect upon a complex and multifaceted understanding of time. Ricoeur submits that time can be linear, nonlinear, mythic, and multidimensional. Historical events are often related in a linear mode. Narration of a story may be linear or nonlinear, with past and future events weaving in and out of the present moment. Mythic time holds the timelessness of story and points to the aporetics of time. Ricoeur (1988:243) writes that there is an "unrepresentability of time, which makes even phenomenology continually turn to metaphors and to the language of myth, in order to talk about the upsurge of the present or the flowing of the unitary flux of time." The narratives of urban China take place within a vastness of time.

This exploration of urban Chinese identity also looks toward the critical hermeneutic work of Ellen Herda. In *Research Conversations and Narrative*, Herda addresses the three research categories for this document: *mimesis*, appropriation, and imagination. Herda discusses the tradition of hermeneutic inquiry and the shift toward ontology. Herda (1999:10) writes:

> When we understand that language is an action that is the medium of our lives, we become connected to others in historical and current communities that have a future. Further, our being in the world is revealed historically in and through language as discourse—a concept in the hermeneutic tradition that implies a relationship with an other.

It is through language that we express thought, create meaning, and define our world. Sometimes new language emerges to create new meaning. Sometimes foreign words are appropriated to express an idea that is not represented within our own linguistic paradigm. In addition, through metaphor, there can be implied meaning or multiple meanings. Herda (1999:21) observes, "Our language reflects our values and priorities." In Chinese, the characters for the word "democracy" are *min* and *zhu*, meaning "people" and "master"—together these create the word for democracy (Gao 2000:125). It is evident that the English word for democracy has a different connotation than the Chinese word for democracy. Yet, in spite of the negative implication of the word "master," the fuller meaning of democracy reaches people in Shanghai and other places. Hans-Georg Gadamer (2003:401) states, "The fact that our desire and capacity to understand always go beyond any statement that we can make seems like a critique of language. But this does not alter the fundamental priority of language."

In *On Stories*, Richard Kearney explores the meaning and significance of the narrative. Kearney's work references the prior work of Paul Ricoeur and further expands our understanding of $mimesis_1$ (past-present), $mimesis_2$ (present-present), and $mimesis_3$ (present-future). Kearney (2002:46) writes, "The retelling of the past is an interweaving of past events with present readings of those events in the light of our continuing existential story." In this passage, Kearney illustrates how our being in time is connected to the past, grounded in the present moment, and also relates to a future story yet to be made manifest. The Shanghainese had a particular identity in the pre-Mao era. This identity changed dramatically after the Communist government assumed power. And it changed again in the post-Mao epoch of Deng Xiaoping and the "Open-Door Policy" (Gao 2000:15). A narrative that knits together this collective identity could offer the Shanghainese a way to make peace with their difficult and tragic past. Furthermore, a new narrative could offer hope to those who feel lost and uncertain in modern, urban China.

Paul Ricoeur, Richard Kearney and other hermeneutic authors attest to the power of the imagination. In *On Paul*

Ricoeur: The Owl of Minerva, Kearney (2004:39) reflects upon the adoption of hermeneutics "as the 'art of deciphering indirect meanings.'" There can be meaning, and there can be implied meaning. A juxtaposition of two contrasting thoughts side by side suggests a different meaning than each thought would have alone. Metaphor also suggests new meaning. There can be various interpretations, as each person has a somewhat different association with particular words and symbols. The Chinese language is rich in nuance and metaphor. Mobo C. F. Gao (2000:77) notes that "a radical is the smallest meaningful unit in a character." Additional brush strokes create a character. Characters can be combined to create words. Thus, there can be many layers of meaning in written Chinese.

In *Truth and Method*, Hans-Georg Gadamer (2003:393) states, "All writing is a kind of alienated speech, and its signs need to be transformed back into speech and meaning. Because the meaning has undergone a kind of self-alienation through being written down, this transformation back is the real hermeneutical task." Words are symbols that become fixed in print. A reader then encounters the text. That reader must then interpret the symbols back into meaning. According to Gadamer (2003:441), Wilhelm von Humboldt was to have said, "To learn a foreign language involves acquiring a new standpoint in regard to one's previous worldview." Encountering a new worldview naturally causes one to reexamine one's own worldview, as there is now a different framework within which one can understand the world (Gadamer 2003:441). Our "language-view" is, in a sense, our worldview (Gadamer 2003:441). And so the question arises: How do young urban Chinese understand the world differently after they have studied English? How do they reinterpret their worldview? Research conversations with urban Chinese shed light on these questions; at times, new aporias unfold. Gadamer's work specifically addresses the research category appropriation.

Chinese Language, Culture and History

This section provides a brief introduction to texts on Chinese language, culture, history, and philosophy to come toward an understanding of urban Chinese identity. Mobo C. F. Gao's (2000) text, *Mandarin Chinese*, provides insight into the Chinese language and thus into Chinese culture. Texts that specifically address Chinese culture are Fox Butterfield's (1982) *Alive in the Bitter Sea* and Colin Thubron's (2004) *Behind the Wall: A Journey Through China*. Other resources address Chinese history, such as *China: Empire and Civilization*, edited by Edward Shaughnessy (2005). This text reviews China's history, culture, art, science, and technological developments. Another comprehensive account of Chinese history is Kenneth Hammond's (2004) *From Yao to Mao: 5000 Years of Chinese History*. Wang Ping's (2000) book, *Aching for Beauty*, offers insight into the lives of Chinese women in the dynastic era. Kathleen Higgins's (2001) text, *World Philosophy*, is a detailed work that illumines the thinking of Confucius, Laozi, Mozi and other great minds in Chinese thought.

In terms of modern history, Julia Kwong's (1988) *Cultural Revolution in China's Schools* examines the trauma and hardship of this ten-year period. The text, *China Urban* by Chen, Clark, Gottschang, and Jeffery (2001), is a compilation of ethnographies in modern, urban China. It discusses the stresses and tensions that are endemic to urban life in China. *China Urban* also specifically addresses the dilemma of the migratory population, those who come to the city in search of work without any rights to education, housing, or health care. Similarly, Gaetano and Jacka's (2004) *On the Move* explores the situations of women who move from rural communities into urban areas in China. Susan Greenhalgh's (2008) *Just One Child* explores the influence of the One-Child Policy in modern Chinese society. Historically, the Chinese placed a higher value on males, and a lesser value on females. In spite of campaigns from 1978 forward to change this mode of thought, there continues to be a preference for a male child even in urban areas. The *Pocket China Atlas* by Stephanie Hemelryk Donald and Robert Benewick (2008) offers current statistical information on China and her population. Witold Rodzinski's (1988) *The People's Republic of China: A Concise Political History* offers in-depth analysis of China's political history and political culture. In *China: A New History*, John King Fairbank and Merle Goldman (2006) provide an historical account of China commencing with imperial autocracy and continuing through the post-Mao reform era.

In addition to the literature above, there are various periodicals that contribute to an understanding of urban Chinese identity. The May 2006 *Smithsonian* article, "A Tale of Two Chinas," discusses the growing gap between the rich and the poor in modern China. Three *Wall Street Journal* articles highlight the problems faced by people in China today. One article, "China's Workers See Thin Protection in Insurance Plans," addresses the lack of adequate health care and rising costs for health care in China. Andrew Browne (2005:1) writes, "The Chinese government's share of total health spending has plummeted. Between 1978 and 2003, private outlays as percentage of total health-care spending rose to 60% from 20%." Chinese people increasingly assume greater responsibility for health care costs, regardless of ability to pay for those costs. In another article, "Chinese Doctors Tell Patients: Pay Upfront, or No Treatment," a child with leukemia is denied treatment unless the parents can raise the funds (Browne 2005:1). A third *Wall Street Journal* article, "Why the Chinese Hate to Use Voice Mail," highlights ubiquitous use of the cell phone in modern China. People do not care to use voice mail because to do so would be redundant. Urban Chinese are ready to answer their phone at any given moment. Rebecca Buckman (2005:1) writes, "People rarely turn off their cell phones in China, even at movies or during funerals." This article has implications for changed culture and changed values. This cell phone culture demands that one respond first to an electronic device, no matter the circumstances of the moment. Relationship to the other is changed. In modern, urban China, emphasis is given to being available to the caller and not to those who are in one's immediate proximity. This change implies that the Shanghainese and other city dwellers may be moving away from the Confucian value of *yi*, appropriateness. Consideration for the other would seem to be relegated to a lower position in China's values.

In 2005, *U.S. News and World Report* conducted an investigative report on China titled, "The China Challenge." In this report, Richard Newman (2005:38) notes that, "for centuries, China was the world's most advanced civilization." The Chinese elite saw themselves as a noble and powerful people, situated at the center of the earth. Mobo C. F. Gao (2000:13) recalls, according to Chinese legend, a Chinese woman named Nuwa "used yellow earth as her raw material and made man and woman and later scattered them all over the world." History and myth recount China's greatness as a culture and a society. This document examines selected narratives that shed light on urban Chinese identity. What is the urban Chinese aim toward the good life? Who are the urban Chinese? What are their hopes and dreams for the future? It is anticipated that the texts identified heretofore will contribute to furthering an understanding of urban Chinese identity. Chapter Four discusses the Research Process for critical hermeneutic research in Shanghai, China.

CHAPTER FOUR

THE RESEARCH PROCESS

Introduction

In this chapter, the primary elements of the research process are discussed in order to provide a basic understanding of how the data were collected and interpreted in light of critical hermeneutic theory. The first part of this section addresses the theoretical foundations for this research, whereas the second part addresses the research process. In research protocol, the following are discussed: entrée into the research site, participant selection, categories, guiding questions, pilot study, language and translation, journal writing, data collection and creation of text, and data analysis and presentation. The protocol for this research adhered to the guidelines set forth in Herda's *Research Conversations and Narrative* (1999:96-100). The findings of this research have implications for Sino-global diplomatic relations and for curriculum development in the field of sinology. This research may contribute to a deeper understanding of urban Chinese identity. Suggestions for further research on urban Chinese identity are proposed in the summary chapter of this document.

Theoretical and Conceptual Background

The primary authors from the critical hermeneutic tradition for this research include Paul Ricoeur, Richard Kearney, Ellen Herda, and Hans-Georg Gadamer. Critical hermeneutic theory is the theoretical framework that provided the basis for this research on urban Chinese identity. Ricoeur (1981:112) describes hermeneutics as "the explication of the being-in-the-world displayed by the text. What is to be interpreted in the text is a proposed world which I could inhabit and in which I could project my ownmost possibilities." Interpretation of a text is subjective, as we come to the text with our own unique history, culture, point in time, and prejudgments. Therefore, interpretation of the text can lead to many different interpretations. Hermeneutics departs from the positivist realm. It is not the aim of hermeneutics to claim that an interpretation is correct or incorrect; rather, there can be many possible interpretations of a text. Individuals can come toward a shared understanding of the meaning of the text through conversation.

Early Anthropologists

Early anthropologists were previously discussed in Review of Literature. These same authors are discussed below in a different context. The work of early anthropologists is, in this section, discussed in terms of text analysis. Victor Turner (1982:122) writes, "When we enter whatever theatre our lives allow us, we have already learned how strange and many-layered everyday life is, how extraordinary the ordinary." Our lives are innately complex as we are continuously moving through time and attempting to create a coherent narrative out of seemingly discordant events. If we examine recent historical events in urban China, we can see that Mao Zedong Thought is juxtaposed with Deng Xiaoping's Open-Door Policy. How can people in China make sense of this movement within extremes?

Perhaps the making sense resides in the extremes, as China is historically a place of stability giving way to change and then moving back to stability.

Levi-Strauss (1978:13) states, "If we look at all the intellectual undertakings of mankind, as far as they have been recorded all over the world, the common denominator is always to introduce some kind of order." We struggle to make sense of and find meaning in our lives. It is through the act of emplotment that we come toward a coherent narrative. Kearney (2002:4) observes, "When someone asks *who* you are, you tell your story." A story takes places within time, and the story can move in and out of a past-present, *mimesis*$_1$; a present-present, *mimesis*$_2$; and a present-future, *mimesis*$_3$ (Ricoeur 1984:53). Ricoeur (1984:25) proposes, "Time must be thought of as *transitory* in order to be fully experienced as *transition*." In reference to Augustine, Ricoeur (1984:25) states, "Time...is never all present at once." Urban China is a place of rapid movement; stillness would seem to be elusive. But even within a still moment, time remains fluid, nonstatic, and multidimensional.

Geertz (1983:234) asserts that the primary question for humankind is "whether human beings are going to continue to be able...through law, anthropology, or anything else, to imagine principled lives they can practicably lead." Kearney (2002:25) submits, "The imaginary liberates the prisoners of our lived experience into possible worlds." In modern, urban China, use of the Internet is monitored by the Communist government. Certain words, such as "democracy," are banned. However, government cannot ban thought. The thought of democracy or the thought of free speech may be alive, even if those words remain unarticulated. In urban China, one must listen carefully to the narratives and observe what is said and what is not said. The absence of speech also tells a story. Ricoeur (1992:320) states that we must "take into account more deeply concealed forms of suffering: the incapacity to tell a story." Ricoeur holds that silencing of the other is a form of violence.

Benedict (1934:14) reflects, "Perhaps...man will destroy himself by...development of intelligence." Humankind has power. We have free will to act justly or unjustly. Herda (1999:7) submits, "The identity of an individual is found in a moral relationship with others." We are always in relationship with the other, whether we pass by the other without a greeting or exchange conversation. In China, a common greeting has been "*Ni chi fan le ma?*" which means "Have you eaten?" This question expresses care and concern for the other. The data show that this expression is fading in modern, urban China. Perhaps the urban Chinese of today are less concerned with sustenance since the standard of living has risen dramatically in recent years. Language changes over time. The Chinese have appropriated some typically Western modes of speech. Research conversations shed light on present-day language, vocabulary, and nuance of expression.

Critical Hermeneutics

This section discusses critical hermeneutic traditions in light of the research process. Critical hermeneutics as discussed by Ellen Herda, Paul Ricoeur, Richard Kearney, and Hans-Georg Gadamer provided the substantive theoretical orientation for this research on urban Chinese identity. The theoretical categories for this work are *mimesis*, appropriation, and imagination. Herda (1999:7) writes, "Critical hermeneutics places the locus of both social and personal change in language and tradition. An essential point in critical hermeneutic participatory research is that it is in language and our tradition that we have our very being." Herda suggests that we must look toward language and culture to understand our ontological condition. In reference to Heidegger, Herda (1999:56) writes that "understanding...constitutes, along with state-of-mind and discourse, the essence of human beings—the being that understands is *Dasein*." As stated earlier, *Dasein* can be generally translated as being or existence. Herda (1999:56) observes that *Dasein* "includes man's conscious, historical existence in the world that by its nature projects into a there beyond its here." The people of urban China live in a present moment. They are influenced by an historic past. Hopes and dreams come alive through the imagination. In *Dasein*, we realize our being-in-time. Herda (1999:56) states, "Being is essentially temporal."

Ricoeur (1984:60) notes that "Augustine set us on the path of an investigation into the most primitive temporal structure of action. It is easy to rewrite each of the three temporal structures of action in terms of this three-fold present." Ricoeur submits that there is a present of the past, to which he designates the nomenclature *mimesis*₁. We are posited in the present moment, yet we are simultaneously in the past via recollection. Ricoeur names the present of the present *mimesis*₂. The present moment contains *mimesis*₁, *mimesis*₂, and *mimesis*₃; and thus *mimesis* is threefold. Ricoeur emphasizes that the present moment is the most tangible, for, in some sense, all we have is the present moment. Ricoeur refers to the present of the future as *mimesis*₃, which is the realm of the imagination. Ricoeur (1984:60) writes, "The actual present of doing something bears witness to the potential present of the capacity to do something and is constituted as the present of the present." Action takes place within time; action punctuates linear time. In 1978, a Democracy Wall was set up in Beijing, on which citizens were encouraged to post political thoughts (Hemelryk and Benewick 2008:29). People were eager to express their ideas on human rights and other issues. However, in 1979, the Democracy Wall was shut down by the Communist regime. Subsequently, in 1989, protests for democratic reform took place at Tiananmen Square. The nonviolent demonstrations at Tiananmen were brutally suppressed by the government (Hemelryk and Benewick 2008:29). The events themselves cannot be changed, but we can attempt to make sense of past events through the configured narrative, which, according to Herda (1999:78), "mediates between individual events and a story taken as a whole."

Kearney (2002:62) states, "Stories bring the horror home to us. They singularize suffering against the anonymity of evil." In present-day China, the horrific events of the Cultural Revolution remain largely unexpressed. It is yet to be seen if these stories will rise to the surface and be told. The Chinese government would need to allow for an open space for the expression of this human suffering. An invitation by the government to express oneself may, justifiably, be viewed cautiously by both rural and urban Chinese. It is apparent from past events, such as the Democracy Wall, that the invitation of free speech may be followed by an unexpected turn of events. The Chinese government must come towards a congruence of speech and praxis in order for trust to develop in modern, urban China. Kearney (2002:62) proposes, "A key function of narrative memory is...empathy." In reference to Kant, Kearney (2002:63) writes that empathy is "a way of identifying with as many fellow humans as possible—actors and sufferers alike—in order to participate in a common moral sense." Testimony has great significance because it does not allow human suffering to be forgotten. Kearney (2002:62) states, "Sometimes an ethics of memory is obliged to resort to aesthetics of storytelling. Viewers need not only to be made intellectually aware of the horrors of history; they also need to experience the horror of that suffering as if they were actually there." Kearney illumines how narrative fiction can hold the truths of our lived experience.

Gadamer (2003:199) states, "The whole continuity of universal history can be understood only from historical tradition itself. But this is precisely the claim of literary hermeneutics, namely that the meaning of a text can be understood from itself. *Thus the foundation for the study of history is hermeneutics.*" Hermeneutics means interpretation of a text. Originally, text was considered to be a written document only. However, hermeneutic inquiry has since expanded to include written text, oral text, and human action, as the latter two can be fixated on the page when penned or typed. Ricoeur (1998:43) writes, "Hermeneutics is the theory of the operations of understanding in their relation to the interpretation of texts." Research conversations are transcribed and become fixed in print. The researcher then appropriates portions of text when something speaks as true or when a pattern emerges. It is the task of the researcher to interpret the whole of the text and to discover its meaning. The narratives of urban Chinese people tell the stories of their lived experiences. These narratives shed light upon urban Chinese identity, and they also lead to new aporias.

Research Protocol

Herda (1999:93) states, "The research protocol is a guideline for thinking about and designing a field-based hermeneutic inquiry project." Research protocol for hermeneutic inquiry offers guidelines; it does not offer specific steps or instructions for designing the research project. The researcher must reflect upon how to design the research project and address the research issue in a way that leads to deeper understanding. Herda (1999:93) emphasizes that hermeneutic participatory research means "learning about language, listening, and understanding." Conversation implies a "to and fro" exchange, as we alternately speak with and listen to the other. Herda (1999:136) writes, "Critical to an understanding of learning in this hermeneutic tradition is the primacy of the dialectic found in hearing. Hearing, as opposed to seeing, is the basis of the hermeneutic experience." In critical hermeneutic participatory research, it is essential that the researcher has an orientation of openness to hear the voice of the other. Critical hermeneutic research protocol (Herda 1999) includes the following: 1) Entrée and Participant Selection, 2) Categories and Questions, 3) Pilot Study, 4) Research Timeframe, 5) Data Collection and Creation of Text, and 6) Data Analysis and Presentation. The following section also provides information on the background of the researcher.

Entrée and Participant Selection

This critical hermeneutic research on urban Chinese identity took place primarily in Shanghai, China. The participants of this research are individuals who reside in, or are originally from, urban areas of China. Participants are in their twenties and thirties, as the focus of this research is on young urban Chinese. The data suggest that there may be a difference between urban research participants who are between the ages of eighteen and twenty-five and those participants who are twenty-six or older. Of the Shanghai research participants, the younger group appeared to have less knowledge of history and less interest in historical events. The pilot study participant, Liu Rui, is a twenty-three-year-old graduate student at the University of San Francisco enrolled in the Organizational Development master's program. The conversation with Liu Rui took place in Carmel, California, in November 2007. A research conversation with Lu Ran, a twenty-seven-year-old University of San Francisco graduate student from China took place in San Francisco, California, in May 2008. Research conversations with an additional nine research participants in Shanghai, China, took place during the months of May and June 2008. In addition to the eleven formal research participants, there were numerous informal research conversations. Informal conversations were recorded in a journal in May and June of 2008.

Individuals who agreed to participate in this research were provided with a letter of invitation and a list of the research questions (see Appendix A). A follow-up letter was also sent to the research participant (see Appendix B). Each participant who was invited to participate was provided with an explanation of research protocol and the nature of their participation.

Specifically, it was explained to each participant that the conversation would be recorded, a text would be created, and the person's name would be used in the research document. Consent forms were delivered to participants prior to the scheduled conversation (see Appendix C). Permission was obtained from the research participant both orally and in writing prior to the conversation taking place. Conversations were conducted in English with the use of some Chinese (Mandarin) words or phrases. Chinese language was transcribed as Pinyin for the conversational text. Pinyin is the form of Romanization for the Chinese language currently used for translation. A copy of the transcript was sent to each research participant for his or her review.

Formal research participants were selected through referrals from professional colleagues and students from urban China. As stated previously, two research participants are international students at the University of San Francisco. The Shanghai research participants include the following: students from East China Normal University; students from Foreign National University; and individuals who are employed in Shanghai. All formal research participants spoke English and Mandarin and were between the ages of twenty-one and thirty-one years old. Informal conversations in Shanghai, China, were primarily with people in their twenties and thirties. The understanding reached in these informal conversations was inscribed in the research journal to provide text for analysis. Traditional anthropological research includes gathering of data from observations, documents, conversation transcriptions, and journal notes.

Figure 1 provides a list of formal research participants for this study. It should be noted that the Chinese surname is listed first and the given name second. The two anonymous research participants have been assigned fictitious English names for purposes of identification within the conversational text and analysis. These two individuals agreed to participate in the research with the understanding that their names would not be identified

in the document. All individuals voluntarily agreed to participate in this research.

Formal Research Participants

Chinese Name	English Name	Age	Occupation
Liu Rui	Vivian	23	Student
Lu Ran	Ryan	27	Student
Wang Xiaoyin	Alice	26	Governmental Officer
Chen Jingjing	Maggie	25	Quality Control Employee
Anonymous	Eric	22	Student
Anonymous	Nicholas	25	Student
Li Shihai	Tom	31	Merchandiser
Zhong Mingyan	Corona	22	Student
Gao Jin	Jimmy	22	Student
Zhou Zijun	Yolanda	21	Student
Shen Lin	Janet	21	Student

Figure 1. Formal Research Participants

Categories and Questions

Research conversations, data collection, and data analysis
were guided by the following research categories: *mimesis*,
appropriation, and imagination, as discussed in Review of
Literature and the theoretical background. These categories
were selected by the researcher in order to come toward a fuller

understanding of urban Chinese identity. Data collection and analysis complied with critical hermeneutic protocol (Herda 1999). The categories identified heretofore are the main theoretical categories for this research. Additional theoretical categories have been included when appropriate to adequately analyze the data obtained for this research.

Guiding questions were used to provide a foundation for opening up dialogue on the issue of urban Chinese identity. Herda (1999:97) states that the purpose of the guiding questions is to create "a context in which a conversation can be carried out." Conversation is not limited to or restricted by the guiding questions. Either the researcher or the research participant may diverge from the guiding questions to introduce a related topic or other matter of significance relating to urban Chinese identity. The pilot study serves to give the researcher an idea of how well the guiding questions engaged the research participant in conversation. Herda (1999:97) suggests that the experience of the pilot study also "creates a practical opportunity to see whether the categories provide the right emphases for the research."

The following guiding questions relate to the research categories selected, although certain questions pertain to one specific research category. These questions were not designed to be answered specifically; rather, they served as boundaries for the data collection. The guiding questions for my research conversations were as follows:

1) What do you think is important to people in China today?
2) What are your thoughts on globalization and its influence on China?
3) Which aspects of modern Chinese life reflect the historic past? (i.e., Confucianism, Daoism, Buddhism, etc.).
4) What problems or tensions do you see in modern China?
5) What changes do you anticipate occurring in China in the near future?
6) What do you hope for your own future?

It may be noted that the guiding questions are intended to offer a stage of preliminary exploration of the research issue, and thus not all questions were asked during each conversation.

Pilot Study

The initial field study was conducted through an hour-and-a-half conversation on November 23, 2007, in Carmel, California (see Appendix D). There was follow-up with the research participant, Liu Rui, through e-mail contact. Liu Rui was provided with a copy of the transcript. Herda (1999:109) notes that the field-testing or "piloting" of one's questions and categories "provides an opportunity to determine whether the questions or guidelines make sense." The field study with Liu Rui confirmed that the guiding questions selected elicit in-depth conversation. The protracted length of the field study conversation indicated that it would be appropriate to reduce the number of guiding questions from ten questions to six questions. The questions selected adequately addressed the categories of *mimesis*, appropriation, and imagination.

Preliminary analysis of the pilot study indicated that there are distinct societal problems in modern, urban China. People in their twenties and thirties in urban China can experience significant pressure and stress from being in a culture of one-child families. Young urban Chinese must provide financially for their own child and, at the same time, support their parents and their spouse's parents. This situation can lead to stress and despair, and also a sense of aloneness since the individual has no emotional support from siblings. Yet, there would also appear to be a sense of hope for a better future in spite of current challenges. The pilot study affirmed that urban Chinese identity is complex and multifaceted, supporting the premise that this research topic was worthy of further inquiry. There was an open orientation and genuine sincerity on the part of Liu Rui in the to-and-fro of the conversation. It is essential that both researcher and participant come toward the conversation with an open orientation to exchange experiences and ideas. It is through authentic conversation that learning can take place in conversation-based analysis.

Research Timeframe

The research process began in November 2007 with a pilot study in Carmel, California. A second research conversation with a different research participant, Lu Ran, took place in San Francisco, California, in May 2008. On-site research with an additional nine research participants was conducted in May and June 2008 in Shanghai, China. For this research, there were twelve recorded conversations with eleven individuals from the fall of 2007 through the summer of 2008. One research participant in Shanghai agreed to a second conversation, which took place in June of 2008.

Data Collection and Creation of Text

Data were collected through twelve formal research conversations that were recorded and transcribed. There was online follow-up with each research participant. A research journal was kept to record observations and reflections. The journal also provided a format to record informal conversations that took place in Shanghai, China. Other resources that contributed to an understanding of urban Chinese identity included books, journals, and magazine and newspaper articles. Recorded conversations were transcribed and fixed into written text. Ricoeur (1981:112) writes, "Hermeneutics can be defined no longer as an inquiry into the psychological intentions which are hidden beneath the text, but rather as the explication of the being-in-the-world displayed by the text."

The text offers a proposed world for interpretation by the reader. Sometimes appropriation takes place: When we take in or appropriate the ideas of the other, we enlarge our world. Herda (1999:129) states that the phenomenon of a fusion of horizons occurs "when we make our own what was once alien." Thus, that which was previously unfamiliar is taken in and claimed as one's own.

Data Analysis and Presentation

The analysis of data followed the critical hermeneutic protocol presented by Herda (1999). Herda (1999:98) states, "Analysis is a creative and imaginative act." The data were analyzed, looking in particular at content, theme, and metaphor. In addition, the themes that emerged with the research categories of *mimesis*, appropriation, and imagination were correlated. This research has abided by the Human Subjects regulations of the Department of Psychology at the University of San Francisco. The boundaries of this research are created by the people who have agreed to participate within the selected categories for data collection and analysis. How the data are understood and interpreted by each reader depends on what each reader brings to this text. I have sent transcriptions and preliminary analysis notes to each conversation partner, thereby each participant has had the opportunity to read his or her own transcript and reflect upon the transcript and the preliminary analysis. Upon reflection, each partner has had the opportunity to delete, add, or change the transcript of what he or she said in the recorded conversation. There was continued dialogue through e-mail correspondence with various research participants, which further contributed to my understanding of urban Chinese identity.

Herda (1999:98-99) identifies the following sequence of actions, that was adhered to in this research, as helpful to data analysis:

- The researcher fixes the discourse in print by transcribing recorded conversations.
- The researcher identifies significant statements, develops themes, and allocates the themes within categories.
- The researcher substantiates the themes with quotes from the conversational text.
- The researcher examines the themes to determine their significance within the theoretical framework.
- The researcher provides the participant with the opportunity of continued discussion to further expand understanding of the topic whenever possible.
- The researcher sets a context for the written discussion by grouping themes and subthemes within the categories.
- The researcher discusses the research issue drawing upon critical hermeneutic theory.
- The researcher identifies significant ideas from the written discussion that offer insight into the research issue.
- The researcher highlights those aspects of the initial findings that merit further study.
- The researcher gives examples of learning experiences for himself or herself, and also offers examples of learning experiences for participants.

The themes identified in the data are as follows: stress and anxiety; erosion of trust, aloneness and alienation; survival; loss of identity and changing identity; and hope for a better future. The first four themes were analyzed through the research category *mimesis*. The theme of loss of identity and changing identity was analyzed through the research category of appropriation. Finally, the theme of hope for a better future was analyzed through the category of imagination. Analysis of the data leads to new understandings of the myriad expressions that are urban Chinese identity. Moreover, data analysis pointed towards areas for further study.

Learning through Hermeneutic
Research and Its Implications

Kearney (2002:81) writes, "One cannot remain constant over the passage of historical time—and therefore remain faithful to one's promises and covenants—unless one has some minimal remembrance of where one comes from, and how one came to be what one is. In this sense, identity is memory." And so it may be said that identity resides in time. The research categories of *mimesis*, appropriation, and imagination all address some aspect of time. *Mimesis* offers a threefold understanding of time; appropriation takes place within time; and imagination propels us into an imagined future. Through this hermeneutic inquiry, a new understanding of urban Chinese identity was revealed.

At times, a fusion of horizons took place for the researcher and the research participant, as each engaged in dialogue and moved toward a tentative understanding of the self and the other. In speaking of Chinese culture, Lu Ran said that "people become very evil in their heart. And there is a dark side that's getting much stronger...I have to protect myself first." He also spoke of the difficulty of finding trusting friendships in the United States. There seemed to be a fusion of horizons for Lu Ran in the realization that the global culture of the twenty-first century is one of rapid change, uncertainty, and mistrust. This researcher came to understand that the United States and China share the theme of alienation. Chen Jingjing reflected on lost dreams: "Sometimes I thought I've become [a] boring person. When I was a student, I had many dreams...but now nothing." This researcher experienced a fusion of horizons listening to Chen Jingjing. There is a common experience the world over: The optimism of youth sometimes gives way to the somber realities of adulthood, a world driven by thoughts of survival and being close to death. The world of the future, the world of dreams, fades and becomes increasingly remote. The world of the present is foremost in our thoughts, and our emphasis is not on the future but on the present. The world of the researcher and that of the participant were both changed through the experience of conversation. Learning takes place for both individuals who take part in the research conversation. Furthermore, good will is furthered when there is a genuine exchange of ideas between or among individuals of different cultures.

Background of the Researcher

I studied Italian at the University of California at Berkeley, and shortly thereafter was an exchange student in Italy and France through the Experiment in International Living in 1979 and 1982 respectively. Subsequently I attended the Monterey Institute of International Studies and studied French, Mandarin Chinese, and International Policy Studies. In 1986, I completed a Bachelor of Arts (B.A.) degree in Political Science at Elmhurst College. Through Monterey Volunteers Overseas, I taught English as a foreign language in Kunming, China, at the Kunming Institute of Technology from 1988 to 1989. In 1995, I earned a Master of Science (M.S.) degree in Human Resource Management from Chapman University. Fluent in Spanish, I have had a career in social services primarily serving a Spanish-speaking clientele prior to commencing doctoral studies. I am committed to fostering intercultural communication, understanding, and cooperation.

Summary

In conclusion, the research process for conversation-based analysis is protracted. It takes place over time. This inquiry into urban Chinese identity draws primarily upon critical hermeneutics as the theoretical framework for data analysis.

The research categories for this study are *mimesis*, appropriation, and imagination. This research sheds light upon the question of who the urban Chinese were, who they are, and who they are becoming. The majority of my research participants were students in Shanghai and individuals who are employed in the city of Shanghai. In addition, two international students at the University of San Francisco, who are originally from urban China, participated in formal research conversations. Thus, this study concentrates on Shanghainese identity with implications for the broader category of urban Chinese identity. It is through the narratives of urban Chinese that we may be able to move toward an understanding of urban Chinese identity. Ricoeur (1992:18) states, "The autonomy of the self will appear... to be tightly bound up with solicitude for one's neighbor and with justice for each individual." We are always in relationship with the other, whether or not we recognize this truth of our being-in-the-world.

CHAPTER FIVE

DATA PRESENTATION AND PRELIMINARY ANALYSIS

Introduction

In Chapter Five, the data are presented and a preliminary analysis of the research findings is offered. Data include formal research conversations, informal conversations, journal entries and field research observations. This discussion is guided by the research categories of *mimesis*, as defined by Paul Ricoeur's theoretical concept of threefold temporality; appropriation, taking in that which was previously foreign; and imagination, our projections into the future of possibilities for our lives in light of our historicity and present-day reality. The themes identified within the research category *mimesis* are twofold: the theme of Aloneness and the Erosion of Trust and the theme of Survival, Materialism and Urban Alienation. The theme associated with the research category of appropriation is Historicity and Shanghainese Identity. The theme of Hope for a Better Future correlates with the research category imagination.

Research conversations for this study rendered a significant amount of data relating to the research category *mimesis*, and less data pertaining to the categories of appropriation and imagination. It was not anticipated prior to conducting field research that the guiding questions would lead to a greater amount of conversational text relating to the research category of *mimesis*; however, both formal and informal conversations naturally generated more text that fit with an analysis drawing upon Ricoeur's threefold time, to which he ascribes the names $mimesis_1$, the past-present; $mimesis_2$, the present-present; and $mimesis_3$, the present-future (1984:53).

The themes Aloneness and the Erosion of Trust; Survival, Materialism and Urban Alienation; Historicity and Shanghainese Identity; and Hope for a Better Future emerge as patterns within the data. The narratives of urban China seek to be told. Kearney (2002:129) writes, "Every human existence is a life in search of a narrative." The voices of the Shanghainese reveal their individual story; at the same time, these voices belong to a greater story. The collective narrative is that of the Chinese and, ultimately, that of humankind. Ricoeur (1988 :105) articulates, "We may say that myth enlarges ordinary time." Thus, while events occur in everyday time, the lived experience of each human being also dwells in the realm of the extraordinary and the mythic.

Presentation of Data and
Preliminary Analysis

Mimesis:

Aloneness and the Erosion of Trust

On May 31, 2008, International Children's Day, I walked around the city of Shanghai and later journaled: "Observed that most people do not smile. However, if you smile or say hello in Chinese, then there is generally a friendly response. One can see that people are very proud of their one child. The children are very well dressed—even to play in the park." Children are cherished in China. The Chinese language denotes hierarchy of sibling relationships. Older sister is *jie jie*, younger sister is *mei mei*, older brother is *ge ge*, and younger brother is *di di*. But, in the one-child culture, there is no more sibling relationship for the majority of families. Maturana and Varela (1987:234) write, "Since we exist in language, the domains of discourse that we generate become part of our domain of existence and constitute part of the environment in which we conserve identity and adaptation." In language, we describe our understanding of the world and disclose our identity as a people.

Hua Yun said, "As one child, we are very lonely." The voice of Hua Yun, a twenty-year-old bookstore clerk, would be heard many times in Shanghai. People in their twenties and thirties express a sense of aloneness amidst the vortex of urban life. There is an entire generation of people who have no sibling and thus no shared family history with a peer. Susan Greenhalgh (2008:59) writes that Jiang Qing, the wife of Mao Zedong, "claimed that birth planning was a 'feminine triviality' (*popo mama de xiaoshi*), literally, a mother-in-law's and mother's small affair." However, others did not share this view. In fact, family planning would come to be a significant issue for people in both rural and urban China. Government Premier Zhou Enlai was in charge of providing for the urban population towards the end of the Cultural Revolution. Zhou was responsible for initiating an ideological shift toward limiting population growth in the 1970s. Greenhalgh notes that Zhou believed that the number of births should correspond with economic growth (2008:59). Greenhalgh (2008:86) documents: It was not until after the Cultural Revolution, in 1978, that "a new constitution made birth planning a constitutional obligation." One-child families were promoted and eventually enforced through social pressure and monetary penalties. Greenhalgh (2008:59) writes, "At the mass level, the use of class struggle techniques to promote birth planning alienated the masses from the party and its birth policies, contributing to the general loss of faith in the leadership and ideology that occurred during the 1970s." The politicization of birth planning eroded the boundary of private and public.

My journal entry of June 4, 2008, states: "We all suffer, hope and dream of a better life. The people of Shanghai search for the good life. Some people seem to feel that the good life will be found in economic well-being combined with having a family. Other people in Shanghai expressed that something has been 'lost.'" The tradition of large families is no longer in modern, urban China. Kearney (2002:81) writes, "One cannot remain constant over the passage of historical time—and therefore remain faithful to one's promises and covenants—unless one has some minimal remembrance of where one comes from, and of how one came to be what one is. In this sense, identity is memory." Shanghainese identity includes remembrance of the past, and also desire to find belonging in the modern family of mother, father and one child; but, there is a sense of aloneness for the one child.

A climate of mistrust is pervasive in present-day urban China. Eric, an undergraduate student at East China Normal University, said, "We have been taught from little child; my father and mother told me do not trust the strangers." Eric spoke extensively of the climate of mistrust in Shanghai, China. He said, "Such as the news in Taiwan, very sensitive question. The words just replaced by all the 'x.' You can't talk the words." Eric stated that governmental censorship also applies to the Internet. In reference to *Wikipedia*, Eric said, "We can't log onto this website because of the great fire wall." Nicholas, a graduate student also studying at East China Normal University, expressed a different view. Nicholas said, "Maybe...our government banned certain words. They have their reason because there are always some people, they want to disturb the harmonious society." Nicholas's view seems to be one that sees governmental censorship as protective of Chinese people. China's history affirms that the influence and presence of foreigners has not always been beneficial to the people of China. Kenneth

Hammond records two historic events that illustrate this: the Opium War of 1839 to 1842 and the 1937 invasion of Japan into China, known as the Marco Polo Bridge Incident (2004:172). Nicholas asserted that trust is present within the family: "In my family…we can say anything about the government, about the people we met." Both Eric and Nicholas's words indicate that relationship with family in urban China is crucial for well-being, as one has a context within which thoughts can be expressed freely. Eric articulated, "I think…freedom is most important for everyone in the world today."

To express ourselves with other human beings is to be fully in-the-world, and this act requires freedom to speak. Ricoeur (1992:320) writes, "We must…take into account more deeply concealed forms of suffering: the incapacity to tell a story." In China today, there remains a silence as to the sufferings of the Cultural Revolution, which took place only a little more than three decades past. Witold Rodzinski (1988:126) writes of the Cultural Revolution, "There was a veritable rampage of terror and vandalism, conducted with complete impunity." The Red Guards, comprised largely of China's youth, harassed and persecuted persons who were thought to be "intellectuals" or "bourgeois." Julia Kwong (1988:64) describes how humiliation was used to attack individuals during the Cultural Revolution: Students "denounced the 'bourgeois intellectuals' before the whole school, paraded them through the streets, shaved their heads, and made them wear placards announcing their crimes." The acts of violence that took place during the Cultural Revolution signify a departure from Confucian tradition. During the dynastic period in China, individuals had revered persons of a higher status in hierarchical relationships. Prior to the Cultural Revolution, one generally deferred to elders and to persons in positions of authority. The Confucian tenet *xiao*, filial piety, illustrates reverence for hierarchy. *Xiao* was sometimes abandoned during the Cultural Revolution, as students would turn in their own mother or father to government officials when the parents did not adhere to the teachings of Mao Zedong. Kwong (1988:5) writes, "Mao emphasized the power of ideology in transforming the individual as well as modernizing the country." Mao's ideology left no room for moderation.

The people of present-day China live with the violent past that is the Cultural Revolution although there is no cohesive narrative to relate these events as a society. On June 4, 2008, I wrote in my journal: "The past is present, but it is usually not articulated or expressed by the Shanghainese. Most people speak of the present and the future." It is incumbent upon the government of China today to create a dialogue about the Cultural Revolution and past sufferings. People could come towards a greater sense of peace and justice through dialogue of past events. It is understandable that, without a specific and true invitation by Communist officials, citizens would be hesitant to speak out on controversial subjects. Silence is a form of suffering. Ricoeur (1992:320) writes, "With the decrease of the power of *acting*, experienced as a decrease of the effort of *existing*, the reign of suffering, properly speaking, commences. Most of these sufferings are inflicted on humans by humans." Lu Ran, a graduate student, said, "People become very evil in their heart. And there is a dark side that's getting much stronger based on the social, one-time people want to meet you. I have to protect myself first. And that person might feel the same way. He has to protect himself. So…We don't really talk real things." The statements of Lu Ran, Eric and Nicholas would seem to indicate an increased sense of alienation and mistrust in modern, urban China.

Survival, Materialism and Urban Alienation

The Shanghainese may not feel safe to speak out, as the political current could shift, and what was previously acceptable could suddenly be rendered unacceptable. There are numerous precursors to this phenomenon in urban China, two examples being the Cultural Revolution of 1966 to 1976 and the Tiananmen Incident of 1989. Hemelryk and Benewick (2008:29) record that in 1978, a Democracy Wall was set up in Beijing where citizens were "encouraged to paste political tracts." Hemelryk and Benewick note, however, that the wall was closed by the government the following year (2008:29). Hemelryk and Benewick document that, subsequently, in 1989, students holding peaceful demonstrations for democratic reform were tragically gunned down by Communist soldiers at Tiananmen Square (2008:29). Although the Tiananmen tragedy occurred in Beijing, the Shanghainese and the rest of urban China heard of this unjust and brutal event.

A majority of Shanghainese make efforts to adhere to established societal norms in their everyday life and hope that sudden change does not unseat a tenuous hold on safety, stability, or relative economic well-being. Herda (1999:10) writes, "We become connected to others in historical and current communities that have a future. Further, our being in the world is revealed historically in and through language as discourse—a concept in the hermeneutic tradition that implies a relationship with an other." The Shanghainese are acutely aware of relationship with the other. Gao Jin, an undergraduate student at East China Normal University, observed, "Harmony is most important in China." In Shanghai, the painter, writer or student may venture outside of established norms, but he or she assumes risk in doing so. One must weigh self-expression against the possibility of persecution. In the *Daodejing*, translated by Roger Ames and David Hall (2003:19), Mencius reflects: "Everything is here in me. There is no joy greater than to discover creativity (*cheng*)." The pull toward self-expression and creativity is profound, and thus silence may give way to voice.

Communist governmental policies and regulations together with cultural values create present-day boundaries for acceptable behavior within urban China. Liu Rui, a graduate student, said, "The policies in China, I think you don't have many freedoms to do whatever you want. What do you say? What do you do? You're just under the control of the government, the leaders. And sometimes even if the law, it doesn't say you can't do this, but we have a very strict moral rule: Everybody is watching you." On May 18, 2008, I made the following journal entry: "China is a mix of old and new." The one-child rule is juxtaposed with the historic tradition of having large families; but, today, the one-child mandate is the prevailing norm. The Confucian tradition of *yi*, or appropriateness, dates back to the sixth century B.C.E. Lu Ran stated, "Confucianism dominates the whole Chinese cultural values." The importance of relationship to the other was, and is, critical in China. *Guanxi* is a word unique to the Chinese language. In the *Oxford Starter Chinese Dictionary*, edited by Boping Yuan and Sally Church (2000:47), *guanxi* translates into English as "connection, relationship or tie." One must foster *guanxi* to survive in modern, urban China. Without *guanxi*, one cannot obtain employment, housing, or perhaps even entrance to the university. Liu Rui said, "In China, it is very important because no matter the quality of the employees, if someone has a strong connection with *guanxi*, very good, then they just hire." Competition is fierce for good jobs in Shanghai and other cities. Lu Ran said, "A lot of people are waiting. A lot of people swarm to the cities. It's like one position; maybe even a hundred people are waiting for the position. If you don't do well, you get fired because they don't care about firing people." The prevailing atmosphere of urban China would appear to be one of pressure, tension and uncertainty. Developing strong relationships with others diminishes anonymity in the vastness of urban life.

The Shanghainese strive to compete through developing connections, learning English, and by going abroad to work or study. Two research participants, Chen Jingjing, a quality control employee, and Wang Xiaoyin, a governmental officer, both expressed an interest in increasing their English language skills as a means of advancement in urban China. Chen Jingjing said that, in the near future, she would like to "improve my ability...

the language skills." Wang Xiaoyin said, "I think improving myself is very important, just like learning English. Then, I want to go to the foreign company and get ideas of the Western company." It is fashionable in Shanghai to appropriate Western ways. In my journal entry of June 4, 2008, I reflected: "Shanghainese have strongly embraced Western fashion and Western technology—the cell phone, e-mail, and text messaging are everywhere. Shanghai fashion celebrates bright colors, stripes, the miniskirt, fishnet stockings and silver high heels. What happened to the Mao suit?" Something is lost and something gained. Research participant Li Shihai, a merchandiser, said, "Some people hate the mobile and cell phones." He said that these phones are "a kind of interruption and also no more private spaces." The cell phone continuously punctuates rare moments of near silence amidst the cacophony of city streets. There is minimal space for solitude and reflection. The current frenzy of ultramodern Shanghai contrasts with traditional China, where quiet conversation and sipping tea were the norm. He Xinyan, a professional tour guide, said of Shanghai, "Even if you stayed from morning to night, everything changes."

Survival amidst rapid change and uncertainty would appear to reside at the root of urban Chinese identity. Liu Rui said, "You can say you have a very pure spirit or something; it doesn't work. Without money you can't live." Chen Jingjing stated, "I think there is a difference between the developed and the developing countries. So, for me, the main problem is survival. I want…no, nothing, just survival." This statement would imply that the lack of economic stability in modern, urban China may create a kind of spiritual vacuum. People do not feel free to pursue interests or to engage in thoughts about the nonpragmatic aspects of being-in-the-world. Zhong Minyan, an undergraduate student at East China Normal University, said, "I have a lot of time, but I can only study, study, study. I think the students in USA or Japan; they can do a lot of things, *zai ke wai* [hobbies, interests]." Li Shihai reflected, "Sometimes I feel the life is meaningless. We just live, open the eyes, just work, go to the company to handle lots of complicated things...There are lots of people who standby. So if you cannot, say, really survive, OK you go. You will be eliminated by someone else very easily." These narratives indicate that a fullness of life is absent from life in modern, urban China.

The Shanghainese search for the good life, and yet the good life would seem to be elusive in urban China. Ricoeur (1992:179) writes, "The 'good life' is, for each of us, the nebulus of ideals and dreams of achievements with regard to which a life is held to be more or less fulfilled or unfulfilled. It is the plane of 'time lost' and of 'time regained.'" Dreams guide us toward something, and when that future time arrives, there can be disappointment or fulfillment. The struggle for survival in contemporary China does not obliterate dreams, but it does consume space within physical time. Ricoeur (1988:22) states, "Narrative poetics needs the complicity as well as the contrast between internal time-consciousness and objective succession, making all the more urgent the search for narrative mediations between the discordant concordance of phenomenological time and the simple succession of physical time." Time goes by and we also concurrently experience time, which may seem slow, speedy, protracted or convoluted. The Shanghainese are fully aware that time is passing as they search for *eudemonia*, a deep and enduring happiness, on this journey we call life.

Research participant Chen Jingjing said, "For our age persons, young persons, the problem is money." She further articulated, "This main problem for me is to get money." Research participant Wang Xiaoyin said, "I want to get a lot of money to support me and my parents and create bright future." Gao Jin stated, "If you want to get a good life, you must earn a lot of money; this is very basic." This is the modern conundrum of the Shanghainese: The pursuit of the material world would seem to be all consuming, leaving little room for deep reflection and sharing time with others. I asked Gao Jin to explain further what she thought the good life included, and she replied, "Loved ones." The pursuit of money would seem to temporarily obscure the meaning that is behind the pursuit of money. In Shanghai, the word money is often articulated at the forefront of conversation. Liu Rui recalled that, during the Cultural Revolution of 1966 to 1976, "at that time, money is evil." Since the Opening-Up period ushered in by Deng Xiaoping, the relationship with money changed. It was again acceptable to pursue economic gain for one's personal benefit, in addition to the benefit of society. However, the move toward a modified market economy has not benefited people equally in urban China. Liu Rui said, "The Opening-Up, it makes a gap between the poor and the rich more and more wide." The poor of urban China may experience non-belonging or alienation from the mainstream of society.

Those who believe that monetary gain is still possible also experience a kind of alienation. Chen Jingjing said, "When I was a student, I had many dreams...but now nothing, just money for me." Kearney (2002:25) writes, "The imaginary liberates the prisoners of our lived experience into possible worlds where they may roam and express themselves freely, articulating things that generally dare not say their names and giving to our inexperienced experience the chance to be experienced at last." Chen Jingjing's dreams still reside in memory, and they are therefore still a part of her identity. Identity is nonstatic; rather, it is constantly changing and unfolding. Chen Jingjing may yet return to hopes, dreams and wishfulness. Heidegger (1971:106) submits, "Time times simultaneously: the has-been, presence, and the present that is waiting for our encounter and is normally called the future." The people of urban China, as all of humanity, are in the present moment, in the past via recollection, and in the future through the imagination. In *Time and Narrative*, Volume I, Ricoeur (1984:53) describes this threefold nature of time as $mimesis_1$ (the past-present), $mimesis_2$ (the present-present), and $mimesis_3$ (the present-future).

In Shanghai, there would appear to be an emphasis placed on seizing the present moment to attain monetary well-being before the potentiality of wealth and thus safety slip away. The people of China remember a past when death was close. The obsession with materialism in modern, urban China is understandable in light of historic famine and deprivation. However, this preoccupation would seem to obfuscate deeper issues of relationship and belonging. Monetary gains would not seem to equate happiness for the Shanghainese. It is possible that the absence of deep relatedness with others creates a feeling of being lost in modern, urban China. Lu Ran said, "China, in old times, people liked to socialize. It's kind of easy to find friends in the old times because...people are pretty stable." Lu Ran's statement illumines the aloneness and alienation that characterize urban China today.

Life in modern, urban China is rife with stress, anxiety, and depression, as people attempt to cope with the difficulties of living in crowded, polluted cities. Hemelryk and Benewick (2008:9) record that Shanghai has 954 skyscrapers and 1.1 million passenger vehicles. Hemelryk and Benewick (2008:9) state that the gross domestic product (GDP) of Shanghai is 1,029 billion yuan, with 51 percent from services and 49 percent from industries. Pollution from industry is a serious problem for China. Ted Fishman (2008:144) writes, "Coal consumption has more than doubled since 1990, and even the world's largest coal producer can barely keep up...China recently surpassed the U.S. in carbon dioxide emissions." The air quality in urban areas is noticeably compromised. Research participant Lu Ran said, "Pollution is getting very serious. If you go to Shanghai...the sky is always gray, and the quality of air is actually pretty horrible. So, pollution, I think, is the first problem." Brook Larmer (2008:152) reflects on China: "This earthly paradise is disappearing fast. The proliferation of factories, farms, and cities—all products of China's spectacular economic boom—is sucking the Yellow River dry." Thus, while China's rapid growth has brought greater economic wealth to city dwellers, it has also brought pollution and an imbalance of nature. Historically, harmony with nature has been integral to Chinese belief, as this concept dates back to the time of Daoism in the sixth century B.C.E. Moss Roberts (2004:29) writes that in the *Yi Jing*, (*The Book of Changes*), *heng* is a hexagram that "stands for renewal after return to the origin, hence, circular movement." The hexagram *heng* acknowledges that it is necessary to replenish the earth, to go back to the source, so that the earth can yield further harvests. Kathleen Higgins (2001:17) states that the Daoists believe that "heaven, earth, and humanity can influence one another." Research participant Liu Rui said, "I think Dao nowadays is fading because it doesn't match the modern society." It could be that Chinese identity is changing: There does not appear to be as strong of a relationship with nature in present-day urban China.

The Shanghainese have few green spaces, and so relationship with nature may be becoming more and more remote over time. Shanghai is densely populated. Research participant Lu Ran described Shanghai in the following manner: "I lived in Shanghai...Every morning, I have to go get on the subway and go to another part of Shanghai. It's very, very crowded—very crowded. Every morning, I feel like it's very painful." Clearly, this statement indicates that Lu Ran experienced significant stress in his daily life in Shanghai. Liu Rui said, "The country, it developed too fast without waiting for the people to adapt to it. So, now, we have so many people who can't find a job, so many people who can't go to hospitals; just too many problems." Liu Rui's statement indicates that change has occurred at a rapid pace in urban China; but, individuals are unable to emotionally adjust to this rapid change, perhaps resulting in a lost identity. Liu Rui said, "I think we are in the process of losing identity because we always feel unsafe, confused."

In the dynastic period, and through the first two decades of Communism, agricultural life was highly valued. However, in recent times, globalization has changed the face of modern, urban China. Lu Ran said, "The people in the country, in the rural places, they want to live in the city because they don't want their kids to be farmers anymore." The city is viewed as a place of opportunity and wealth, even though migrants are at a distinct disadvantage in the city. Lu Ran said, "We call this people *ming gong*, this means rural-urban immigrants." Lu Ran observed that migrants from rural China "have to take the most tiring jobs, like cleaning jobs, babysitting jobs." These rural-to-urban migrants often come to the city without legal permits, and therefore, they are not entitled to housing and educational benefits for their children. The gap between rich and poor becomes deeper still, as more and more people flood to the cities, straining existing resources. There may be a lack of understanding and empathy for the migrant peoples, as one sometimes hears the pejorative nomenclature, "the floating people."

The stress of city life can lead to anxiety and depression for many in the urban setting. Lu Ran said: "I have most of my friends live in Shanghai. They have their own stress, anxiety, depression sometimes. And sometimes they even go to doctors for help because they feel too much pressure for their life, and they are afraid of losing their jobs because they do not own the mortgage of their house." The modified market economy allows for individuals to buy private property in Shanghai today. Lu Ran noted that real estate is a significant issue for people in urban China. He said, "People start buying houses like crazy. It never happened before. So, the prices of houses are going really high, every minute, every second." Lu Ran communicated a sense of hopelessness amidst the stress and angst of city living. He seemed to feel that the plodding, predictability of life in urban China would be suffocating for him. The pursuit of things would leave little room for creativity, imagination, and variety. Lu Ran said, "I can see all my life through the people around me and I feel pretty scared. I feel like, wow, this is going to be that's my life." The present-present would seem to be unsatisfying, and the present-future anxiety ridden for Lu Ran and others in urban China. *Luan*, chaos, always lurks in the narrative of China's past. *Luan* is a significant word in Chinese culture, representing the flux of *yin* and *yang*. Stability gives way to change. Well-being of the present moment can readily give way to discord and chaos.

Our language reflects our being-in-world. It is through language that we describe our world. Gadamer (2003:441) writes, "If every language is a view of the world, it is so not primarily because it is a particular type of language (in the way that linguists view language) but because of what is said or handed down in this language." At times, language seems inadequate to convey intended meaning; rather, it seems an approximation of meaning. Gadamer (2003:401) submits, "We must rightly understand the fundamental priority of language…Indeed, language often seems ill suited to express what we feel…The fact that our desire and capacity to understand always go beyond any statement that we can make seems like a critique of language. But this does not alter the fundamental priority of language." Perhaps new language will emerge in modern, urban China to describe the feelings of stress, angst and being lost. In this manner, the Shanghainese can begin to describe their world and define their present-day identity.

Appropriation:

Historicity and Shanghainese Identity

The dynastic epoch of China had distinct characteristics and a definitive identity, and this is the historical identity of urban China. Influences include Daoism, Confucianism, and Buddhism. However, the modern era has also been influenced by globalization and Communism, specifically Mao Zedong Thought. Thus, present-day identity includes the historical past, recent past, present, and a future not yet realized. Shanghai is now a place of high fashion, cutting edge technology, and entrepreneurship. Not long ago, Shanghai culture reflected the political and social ideals of Maoism. Liu Rui described dress during the Cultural Revolution as follows: "People wear uniform...There are maybe only three colors of clothing: gray, blue, and maybe black. All the women, they can't have long hair." Liu Rui elaborated, "Everybody is extremely the same, the status, no wealth." Past and present are both encompassed in Shanghainese identity. But, there appears to be a lostness to this identity, as the Shanghainese struggle to find congruence between who they are now, who they have been, and who they are becoming. Li Shi Hai said, "Maybe Chinese people, they really can see through something, but they do not want to speak out. We say we can see through, but we cannot say through." Thoughts are powerful, articulated or unexpressed; these are the seeds of imagination and the beginning of a new narrative for China.

The Shanghainese, perhaps more than any other people in China, have appropriated foreign thoughts, ideas, and manner of dress. Chen Jingjing said, "Many young people want to copy... Western things, Western habits." The style of the Shanghainese is a blend of East and West. Chen Jingjing expressed her belief that some Western influences may not be good for young people in China. She said, "Western persons' open sex, maybe influence the young person...My parents think foreign person is too open. It's too sexy. It's bad." The implication of these statements is that some people in urban China view Western influences with caution and trepidation. An undergraduate student at Shanghai International Studies University, Shen Lin, echoed this sentiment when she said, "After the Opening-Up, we maybe lost many things, the foreign things coming and they bring us maybe violence and sex, not very good." Shen Lin noted that the Chinese way is to follow a path of moderation. She said, "When we do one thing, we will choose the compromised way and we not choose extreme way." Also an undergraduate student at Shanghai International Studies University, Zhou Zijun, said, "People in China love peace, no war." Moderation resides at the core of Chinese identity. Shanghainese garb may point toward appropriation of all that is Western, yet the narratives of Chen Jingjing, Shen Lin and Zhou Zijun reveal an underlying truth. The Shanghainese retain a belief in the Middle Way.

To appropriate is to take in as one's own that which was previously foreign. Ricoeur (2004:107) writes, "The verb 'to appropriate' plays on the possessive and on the verbs signifying to own and to impute to oneself." The Shanghainese continuously encounter foreign products and foreign ideas. Appropriation only occurs when the Shanghainese strongly identify with that value or idea. Liu Rui said, "I hope and many people hope that we can be more free to move around the whole country or even move to other countries." She also said, "Some people don't work [hard], but they earn a lot...We just want this society to be more equal." Liu Rui's statements indicate a strong desire for greater freedom and justice in modern, urban China. The concept of freedom has been strongly appropriated by many in Shanghai. Identity of the Shanghainese is changing, as they sift through that which is to be kept, and that which is to be discarded, of foreign ways.

Imagination: Hope for a Better Future

The people of urban China hope and dream of a better future. Shen Lin said, "I hope for a peaceful life...good family, and go through my life meaningfully." Zhong Mingyan said, "My future, I think the most important the health of my family." Shen Lin and Zhong Mingyan's statements indicate that valuing family remains at the core of urban Chinese identity. Nicholas said, "I hope I can learn to feel humanity. I can learn all the people... have a very good will to help each other." The statements would indicate that the concept of well-being for the Shanghainese is bound up with care for family and, perhaps to a lesser degree, for others in the community. Ricoeur (1992:225) writes, "We have always known the difference between persons and things: we can obtain things, exchange them, use them; the manner of existing of persons consists precisely in the fact that they cannot be obtained, utilized, or exchanged." In present-day urban China, there appears to be an obsession with the accumulation of goods; but behind the pursuit of material wealth lies the desire to create a safeguard from hardship and death. It is not the things in themselves that are desired, but rather the promise of a better life. Integral to urban Chinese identity is a nearness to death.

There appears to be a desire to have more choice in modern, urban China. Lu Ran described life in urban China as "linear." He commented on how there are many expectations for people in their twenties and thirties in China: to have a profession, to live in one place, to marry and have a child. Liu Rui also spoke of the expectations of others. She said, "People say Chinese women have a lot of freedom...but the truth is we don't have choice." Liu Rui indicated that women must work outside of the home, even if the woman's preference would be to stay at home after giving birth to a child. Liu Rui said, "A man is supposed to get married with a woman whose status is lower than him." For this reason, Liu Rui indicated that she would not pursue a doctorate degree. Liu Rui reflected, "If you are a woman doctor, what kind of man you can find? Too limited." In urban China, as in other parts of the world, choice is mitigated by tradition and societal norms. The Confucian tenets of *yi*, appropriate conduct, and *xiao*, filial devotion, remain strong values in contemporary urban China. Hammond (2004:39) writes, "In the post-Communist age, many elements of traditional society have begun to reemerge." Those aspects of Chinese belief that lay dormant return to the surface in the modern era. Ricoeur (1981:294) writes, *"We belong to history before telling stories or writing history."* In other words, we come into history at a particular point in time, to a particular place, with established cultural norms.

Imagination opens up new possibilities and may depart from the bounds of prejudgment, expectation or societal norms. Lu Ran said, "I don't feel happy anymore. I don't want to go through the same way. I have to have change because life is really short." Lu Ran seemed unsure of what his unprescribed path would be, but, in his imagining that his life could be different, the possibility of living differently unfolds. Ricoeur hypothesizes that fiction is referential back to our lived experience. Ricoeur (1981:296) states, *"The world of fiction leads us to the heart of the real world of action."* Our imagination relies upon past images and experiences to project into the future. Ricoeur (1981:293) writes that, in some sense, *"there is only a history of the potentialities of the present."* The present moment is fecund and can give way to new, imagined ways of being and acting in the world. Shanghainese identity includes a lived past, a present ontology, and hopes and dreams for a better future. The narratives of the selected research participants indicate that the young people of urban China wish to support and honor their parents. At the same time, the young people of Shanghai seek to have more choices in their lives. They also seek to have greater freedoms of speech and movement.

Summary

Formal research conversations, informal conversations, journal entries and field observations in Shanghai, China, all contribute to a deeper understanding of urban Chinese identity. The themes that emerge from the data include: Aloneness and the Erosion of Trust; Survival, Materialism and Urban Alienation; Historicity and Shanghainese Identity; and Hope for a Better Future. Critical hermeneutic theory provided the theoretical lens with which to conduct preliminary analysis of the data. The research categories employed for data analysis in Chapter Five were *mimesis*, appropriation, and imagination. Hammond (2004:39) writes, "China has undergone dramatic and often traumatic change in the modern age." The data indicate that there seems to be a resultant confusion for the young people of Shanghai. There appears to be a sense of lost identity for the Shanghainese. The young people of modern, urban China attempt to make sense of the stated ideal of Communism juxtaposed with the reality of a modified market economy. There is a false myth in urban China, namely, that the pursuit of wealth will lead to well-being; however, a ubiquitous state of malaise permeates urban life and roundly contradicts this claim. The economic situation of present-day Shanghai is but one influence on identity. Other influences include traditional modes of being, appropriated beliefs, and imagined worlds for the future.

Who are the Shanghainese? In Chapter Six, a secondary analysis of the data will be conducted to delve further into this inquiry.

CHAPTER SIX

SECONDARY ANALYSIS

Themes and Implications

In Chapter Five, a preliminary analysis of the data was presented. In Chapter Six, a secondary analysis of the data is presented, drawing further upon critical hermeneutic theory to come toward a deeper understanding of Shanghainese identity. This secondary analysis is also guided by the research categories of *mimesis*, appropriation, and imagination. *Mimesis* offers a means to examine the data in terms of Paul Ricoeur's theory of threefold time, namely, the past-present, present-present and present-future. Appropriation provides a theoretic lens to explore that which has been taken in and kept over time from previously foreign ways and thoughts, and then woven into the fabric of Shanghai's culture. Finally, the research category imagination guides an analysis of the research participants' hopes and desires for their future. Chapter Six concentrates on themes that were found to repeat within the data, and also highlights the implications of each of these themes.

One prominent theme in my research conversations is that the Shanghainese strongly value stability. Attaining and keeping stability are essential to well-being in urban China. One implication for this research could be a need for the government to implement policies for more measured economic growth together with increased social services. Research participants frequently cited feelings of stress, anxiety and a sense of alienation in urban society. Another consistent theme in my research conversations is that the Shanghainese highly value moderation; however, a collective narrative to address the extreme violence of the Cultural Revolution is absent from public dialogue. There appears to be a need for the knitting together of past and present events into a cohesive narrative of urban Chinese identity. The government could initiate sincere and open dialogue of the traditions of the dynastic period, the hardships of early Communism, the present-day modified market economy, and the influence of globalization. A collective narrative of the Shanghainese could help to heal past wounds, make sense of contradictions, and open the way for deeper relationship and trust within urban Chinese society. Finally, a third theme that emerges from my research conversations is the desire for greater freedoms within Chinese society. The Shanghainese are keenly aware of different ways of being around the world in spite of Internet monitoring by the Communist government, and other restrictions placed on media sources in China (i.e., radio, television, literature, and news in printed format). The desire for expanded freedoms suggests the need for the government to listen to the voices of urban China, as they call out for freedoms intrinsic to, as phrased by Heidegger (1962:203), our being-in-the-world.

Secondary Analysis of the Data

Mimesis:

The Significance of Stability in Chinese Culture:
Past, Present and Future

The desire for stability has long been embedded in Chinese culture due to periods of famine, political upheaval, and, more recently, the suffering that has occurred during the Communist era. In *Heart of the Dragon*, Alasdair Clayre (1984:227) cites a poem, written by a Northern Song dynasty poet, Su Dongpo (1036-1101), that was "put into the mouth of a farmer's wife":

My tears are all cried out, but rain never ends.
We sold the ox to pay taxes, broke up the roof for kindling;
We'll get by for a time, but what of next year's hunger?
Officials demand cash now—they won't take grain;
The long north-west border tempts invaders.
Wise men fill the court—why do things get worse?
I'd be better off bride to the River Lord.

Su Dongpo's poem well-illustrates the desperation of the farmer's wife who contemplates taking her own life as she finds herself without further resources to survive. Ricoeur (2004:66) writes, "The phenomenological notion of trace...is constructed on the basis of *being-affected* by an event, becoming its witness after the fact through narration." Thus, narration, both oral and written text, provides testimony to lived experiences. Remembrance of past events carries forward into the present essential truths of a person's being-in-the-world, and that person is not forgotten. In my journal entry dated May 22, 2008, I wrote, "Lawrence [fictitious name] told me that during the Great Leap Forward people were starving and his grandfather died of starvation." I was deeply moved by Lawrence's trust in telling me, a foreigner and stranger, of the loss of his grandfather in this tragic manner. I will never forget the story of Lawrence's grandfather, even though I do not know his grandfather's name.

The aim of the Great Leap Forward of 1958 to 1959 was to increase industrial production in urban areas, but also to increase agricultural production on collectivized farms through-out the countryside. There was pressure from the Communist government to meet or exceed quotas, which resulted in crop production rates being grossly exaggerated. This phenomenon, coupled with challenging weather conditions in those years, lead to widespread starvation. Kenneth Hammond (2004:145) notes that there are "figures ranging up to 20 million people dying as a result of the food crisis during the Great Leap Forward." On May 16, 2008, I wrote in my journal details of an informal conversation with a Shanghainese woman, Wang Zhuong Fang. I inquired about the current usage of the phrase, "*Ni chi fan le ma?*" [Have you eaten?]. This phrase, which reflects the historic past, was still commonly used in the late 1980s. Wang Zhuong Fang told me that the Shanghainese now simply say, "*Ni hao*" [Hello] as a greeting, and that "the other is outdated." Wang Zhuong Fang's statement would seem to suggest that concern for the availability of food has become less acute in modern, urban China. Gadamer (2004:63) writes, "We are always already at home in language, just as much as we are in the world." The language of Shanghainese youth would seem to reside more in present-day relative wealth, and only remotely refer to the realm of past sufferings. Of all my conversations in Shanghai, formal and informal, Lawrence was the only person to initiate a discussion of the Cultural Revolution.

During the Cultural Revolution of 1966 to 1976, Shanghai society as it existed was turned "upside down." Prior to the Cultural Revolution, Shanghai had flourished in the arts, excelled in international trade and commerce, and often appropriated foreign ways. However, during the Cultural Revolution, teachers in Shanghai were considered to be "intellectuals," anyone with a modicum of wealth was labeled "bourgeois," and those who had affiliations with foreign persons or foreign companies were vilified as "Capitalist Roaders." Nien Cheng (1986), a Shanghainese woman who survived the Cultural Revolution, offers testimony of her experience in her book, *Life and Death in Shanghai*. Nien Cheng (1986:319) recounts a day in prison:

I felt very weak. My eyes could no longer focus, and the usual sound of prison activities seemed to grow fainter and fainter. That night, I again sat on the bed, leaning against the wall with my hands crossed to hold the handcuffs with my fingers in an effort to reduce their weights. Though I shivered with cold, I no longer had the strength to get up and walk around the room.

Nien Cheng (1986:407) had worked for a foreign company, and she was accused of being a "spy for the imperialists." Nien Cheng faced the perplexing quandary of not being able to confess a crime that she did not commit. Nien Cheng was imprisoned in solitary confinement, interrogated and tortured, for nearly seven years (1986:1). After the Cultural Revolution ended, Nien Cheng was released from prison to learn that her only child, Meiping, a talented student of the cinematic arts, had committed suicide. Meiping had jumped from a window on Nanjing Road while being questioned by the Revolutionaries (1986:368).

Are the sufferings and tragedies of the distant and recent past unfamiliar to the young people of modern, urban China? Research participant Lu Ran said in reference to people in their late teens and early twenties: "They don't know the historical events that happened during the past...like the Cultural Revolution, 1989 Tiananmen Square protest. They have no idea." Lu Ran's statement would indicate that the young people of urban China may not be fully exposed to knowledge of recent historic events in China. Open discussion of the Great Leap Forward, the Cultural Revolution, and Tiananmen would seem to be tacitly taboo within Chinese society. The older generation, comprised of mothers, fathers, and grandparents, naturally hope for their one child or one grandchild to be safe and to excel in society. To gain advantage in modern, urban China, one ought to adhere to the political beliefs of the current Communist regime, a leadership that emphasizes economic gains and reclaiming a position of high status for China within the global arena.

Extreme hardships were experienced by people in China in the not-too-distant past, and it is understandable that the older generation seeks to protect the younger, in spite of the psychological schism that this may create. The silencing of a people's history may create a feeling of incompleteness or fragmentation in the present, and many questions go unanswered for the young people of China. In my research conversations, the majority of research participants avoided any discussion of historic events that preceded the leadership of Deng Xiaoping and the Opening-Up period. As Lu Ran said, the younger generation does not appear to know China's historical past in detail. Shanghainese in their late teens and early twenties perhaps have a vague awareness of past trauma, yet they avoid such discussion in order to remain within the bounds of political correctness.

The past has implications for the present and future. Ricoeur (2004:89) writes, "The duty of memory is the duty to do justice, through memories, to an other than the self." Through public remembrance of past events, present-day leaders of China have the opportunity of giving testimony to the lives of people who suffered or perished during the Great Leap Forward, the Cultural Revolution, or at Tiananmen. A full narrative of the past need not uproot present-day stability in urban China; rather, the story that is China has the potential to bring about deeper fulfillment and a sense of belonging for the Shanghainese. But, for the truth to emerge, the Chinese government would need to move away from the stance that past events represent a threat to nationalism. Herda (1999:76), citing the theoretical work of Ricoeur, states, "*Mimesis*$_1$ creates the prefigured life, our traditions, assumptions, goals, and motives." The research conversations in this study imply that there is an incompleteness to present-day urban identity: From the vantage point of Shanghainese youth, the past is largely vague, untouchable.

Ricoeur observes that it is the ontological nature of humankind to move in and out of remembrance, imagination, and existing in the present moment (1984:60). The present moment is the most tangible, and in some sense the most real, for it is happening now. Ricoeur (1984:25) brings to light the understanding that "time…is never all present at once." Ricoeur (1984:25) describes time as "transitory," as the present moment continuously gives way to a new moment in time. The hold on the present is fleeting, and many of the selected research participants expressed a preoccupation with earning money now, in these relatively prosperous times. Chen Jingjing said, "I have to save money. I don't want to. I just I have to do it." Eric said that, even though he was only a junior in college, he was already looking for an internship. He said, "I want to make money earlier to support my family." Liu Rui said, "I think the most important thing is just making money because life in China now is getting harder and harder." Li Shihai communicated that, although he doesn't care for a "dull life," he does prefer the stability that earning money brings. The statements by Chen Jingjing, Eric, Liu Rui, and Li Shihai suggest that there is concern that present-day well-being may give way to something else, something unknown, perhaps something horrible.

In my conversation with Liu Rui, I noted that, in China's history, there have been periods of famine. I said, "I think that this is one of the reasons why there has been a focus on earning money and people think about survival more than in countries where it is plentiful, it has been plentiful." I elaborated, "I think that this is part of Chinese identity, this need to survive and to be safe…this is very strong in Chinese thinking." Ricoeur (1984:64) describes the present-present, or *mimesis$_2$*, first, as "a synonym for narrative configuration, second, as an antonym to historical narrative's claim to constitute a 'true' narrative.'" Ricoeur highlights mankind's desire to emplot, create concordance, to tell a cohesive story. We human beings try to make sense of our present-day lives in light of our past and in light of the myriad possibilities for our future. In the present moment, we quite naturally reflect upon our precarious existence as we move through phenomenological time. Ricoeur also makes clear that the recounting of history may or may not correlate with truthfulness of past events. Who is telling the story? Is there an ethical aim to accurately represent past events? Is there an orientation to honor and remember those who have gone before us? The story of the Shanghainese is one of creativity, innovation, boldness, suffering and tragedy, to then rise again like the phoenix. Li Shihai said, "We Chinese people have a saying, *long feng chong xiang* [double happiness]...together with phoenix and dragon and their help...everything is lucky."

Death has always been close to the people of China, and so the word *yunqi*, luck, has great significance in Chinese culture. All of humankind is vulnerable. However, the history of China is unique, and events past include natural disasters, food shortages, economic instability, radical political change, extreme hardship, and tragic loss of life. The Shanghainese, even the younger generation, would seem to have an awareness of nearness to death. Kearney (2002:129) writes:

> Our very finitude constitutes us as beings who...are born at the beginning and die at the end. And this gives a temporal structure to our lives which seek some kind of *significance* in terms of referrals back to our past (memory) and forward to our future (projection). So, we might say that our lives are constantly interpreting themselves—pre-reflectively and pre-consciously—in terms of beginnings, middles and end (though not necessarily in that order).

It would seem that the fear that past hardships may suddenly resurface lies just beneath the surface of urban Chinese thought. The data imply that the Shanghainese hope to stave off hardship, enjoin the good life, and pass on to successors a sense of stability and well-being. As stated previously, maintaining stability, understandably, has great significance to the Shanghainese.

The Shanghainese hope for change, such as greater freedom of speech and expanded personal rights, but they hope for gradual, peaceful change and for the overall betterment of society. No research participant spoke of inciting protests or overthrowing the government. Nicholas said, "I know I'm Chinese. So, this is my country. I love my country." In terms of his future, Nicholas said, "I want to learn. I want to study. I want to know more about the world." Herda (1999:78) writes of Ricouer's *mimesis*$_3$ that the present-future is "an imaginary world we might inhabit." Shen Lin reflects this concept when she said, "I hope to have a peaceful life…have a good family, and go through my life meaningfully," as does Zhou Zijun who communicated hopes for "a nice house with a garden, a husband who loves me…a lovely child, and some friends." Eric's idea of the years to come is expressed when he said, "I think what I seek is to have a good life, just live happier…We can be anyone's friend." The articulated hopes and dreams of Shen Lin, Zhou Zijun, Nicholas and Eric suggest that family, friendship, and deep relatedness with others are important values for the Shanghainese. Eric lamented, "In Shanghai, everyone is an island." In my research conversations, formal and informal, many people spoke of a sense of loneliness in their lives, and the desire for closer relationship with others. This desire for greater relatedness is situated within a particular worldview that is open to new ideas, to appropriate new ways of being and doing.

Appropriation:

Globalization, Historicity and the Middle Way

The data suggest that the value of moderation dwells at the core of Shanghainese identity. Shen Lin said, "We choose the middle road." Li Shihai said, "Every point has two sides." Li Shihai additionally said, "The Chinese people are very sensitive…We don't want to hurt others directly [in speech]." The words of Li Shihai would suggest that consideration is given to others when articulating thoughts, and silence is employed when words could cause harm to others. The desire is strong to maintain positive relationships. The word "harmony" is often heard in Shanghai today. Eric communicated his belief that integral to the good life is "a very harmonious society." The idea of harmony, or balance within nature, has roots in Daoist thought. Kathleen Higgins (2001:28) states, "The fundamental Daoist aim is to attune oneself with the Dao, the natural flow of the world." During the time of my field research from May to June 2008, I found the people of Shanghai, with few exceptions, to be polite, gracious and gentle in their manner.

Present-day Shanghainese identity has many influences. Andrew Forbes (2007:26-43) observes that Shanghai's history includes the dynastic period (2100 B.C.E. to 1912 C.E.); Colonial Rule (1842 to 1912), overlapping the rule of the Qing dynasty; the early Chinese Republic (1912 to 1927); the rise of the Chinese Communist Party in 1921; the Japanese Invasion and Chinese Civil War (1927 to 1949); and the declaration of the People's Republic of China (1949) followed by the era of Communism through the present day. These distinct periods all contribute to the complexity of Shanghainese identity. There would seem to be a sense of confusion within Shanghainese identity today, as the people of Shanghai attempt to make sense of disparate events within time. It may be that the public world of modern Shanghai has an incomplete narrative to tell the story of the Shanghainese. Ricoeur (1988:249) writes, "Narrative... belongs to the ethical field in virtue of its claim—inseparable from its narration—to ethical justice." A full and complete narrative of the Shanghainese has the potential to bring forth an understanding of who the Shanghainese were, who they are now, and who they are becoming.

In the early 1900s, artistic expression abounded in Shanghai. Harper, Pitts and Mayhew (2006:29) write, "The first cinema opened up in Shanghai in 1908" and subsequently reached its peak in the 1930s. The authors (2006:29) recall, "Hollywood stars such as Marlene Dietrich, Katharine Hepburn, Claudette

Colbert and Greta Garbo were household faces in 1930s Shanghai." Harper, Pitts and Mayhew (2006:26) observe that, "in the 1920s and '30s Shanghai was a publishing industry hub and home to a vibrant literary scene." Writers such as Mao Dun, Lu Xun, Zhang Ailing, and Ding Ling all wrote works that reflected Shanghai's culture of the time (2006:26). Harper, Pitts and Mayhew (2006:31) write, "*Huju* is Shanghainese opera, sometimes called flower drum opera. It is performed in the local dialect and has its origins in the folk songs of Pudong." This artistic past would seem to be almost forgotten in the Shanghai of today.

Research conversations indicate that the present-day focus of the Shanghainese is on commerce, international trade, and working hard to take part in Shanghai's wealth. But, then, it must be remembered that this time of relative wealth follows a period of extreme suffering. Witold Rodzinski (1988:121) writes that, during the Cultural Revolution, "some of the Red Guard units… quickly degenerated into a bunch of vicious thugs; for an eyewitness there was a startling and shocking resemblance between their behaviour and that of Nazi storm-troopers." Julia Kwong (1988:114) observes that there was a form of psychological tyranny during the Cultural Revolution:

> To play it safe…teachers used mainly government documents or Mao's works as teaching materials. Teachers taught passages from Mao's works and told stories about Mao and about the heroes who followed in his footsteps. Classrooms across China reverberated with Mao's words: students read, recited, and sang them.

During the Cultural Revolution, foreign music was banned, foreign books were burned, and any thoughts of things foreign dared not be articulated. For the talented and adventurous Shanghainese, the repression that occurred during the Cultural Revolution may have seemed surreal, other worldly. Many tried to survive, clinging to the hope that time would pass and that they would wake up from the nightmare that was the Cultural Revolution. But suffering leaves an imprint. One cannot forget such extreme hardship. Today, perhaps the older Shanghainese quietly reflect upon past hardships and acquiesce to the silencing of the past in favor of relatively peaceful and prosperous times. The youth of Shanghai ask few questions, as surely, they can glean that to do so would be to disturb a certain equilibrium. Moderation was valued in antiquity, suffocated during the epoch of Maoism, and reclaimed in the post-Mao era. Moderation, it would seem, has long been an undercurrent of Chinese culture.

Globalization adds yet another layer to Shanghainese identity. Fareed Zakaria (2008:113) observes, "Culture...does not exist in a vacuum." Culture and identity are closely intertwined. Andrew Forbes (2007:26) writes, "The annals of China's past reveal Shanghai's development from a tiny fishing outpost more than a thousand years ago to China's greatest and most developed city by the start of the 21st century." It is most apparent in Shanghai today that the city's character is cosmopolitan in nature, and the Bund district perhaps exemplifies this more than any other area of Shanghai. Harper, Pitts and Mayhew (2006:104-107) note that Shanghai's Bund district is home to Jardine Matheson, "which became one of Shanghai's great *hongs* (trading houses)"; the Russian consulate; Pudong Development Bank; Armani clothiers; and an Evian spa. Various foreign languages can be heard amidst the glistening edifices of Shanghai, to include French, Spanish, Italian, Russian, Japanese, and English. Of course, *Shanghaihua* (Shanghainese) and *putonghua* (Mandarin Chinese) permeate the city.

Research conversations indicate that the Shanghainese welcome the economic growth that globalization brings, yet, at the same time, the Shanghainese hold tight to their own ways of being. The data suggest that the Shanghainese are indeed fascinated by Western culture, and they continue to value and practice *xiao*, filial piety, and *yi*, appropriate conduct. The Shanghainese continuously encounter foreign ways and foreign ideas, and it is they who then individually decide whether that particular thought or mode of being fits with their own unique identity. Ricoeur (1981:185) writes:

> "Appropriation" is my translation of the German term *Aneignung*. *Aneignen* means "to make one's own" what was initially "alien." According to the intention of the word, the aim of all hermeneutics is to struggle against cultural distance and historical alienation. Interpretation brings together, equalizes, renders contemporary and similar.

Ricoeur highlights an important aspect of appropriation: The Shanghainese must evaluate, weigh, and consider the worldview of the other in order to arrive at their own decision as to whether or not that particular concept or mode of being fits with their own identity. Thus, there is an interplay of exposure to foreign ideas and appropriation, or, alternatively, the decision not to take in the culturally strange and foreign concept. Research participant Chen Jingjing said, "The great part I think is that many top technologies come here." Chen Jingjing expressed that the influx of foreign companies into Shanghai brings more jobs and thus more opportunity. Shen Lin said, "Foreign things are coming and they bring us violence and sex...not very good." Shen Lin spoke of the influence of foreign films in particular. She said, "Every [foreign] movie I see there is sex, violence in it. In our traditional thoughts, for example, violence, these things do not always appear on our screen, in our movies...It's a big shock, but now I have accepted it." Shen Lin's words suggest that she accepts the exposure to Western media and its accompanying values, but she prefers to keep traditional Chinese beliefs. The data indicate that the Shanghainese have appropriated Western fashion, technology, and free market economic principles to the degree permitted by government. However, Shanghainese culture continues to value traditional Chinese modes of being, such as modesty, delicacy in speech, and temperate action.

The xenophobia so prevalent during the Cultural Revolution would seem to be forgotten in China today. Research participant Lu Ran said, "Right now, China is in a very interesting position...It's still opening. It seems pretty welcoming of other people coming to China." Lu Ran's words suggest that, at present, there is momentum toward intensifying Deng Xiaoping's concept of Opening-Up. Fareed Zakaria (2008:89) writes:

> Deng Xiaoping gave a speech that turned out to be the most important in modern Chinese history. He urged that the regime focus on economic development and let facts—not ideology—guide its path. "It doesn't matter if it is a black cat or a white cat," Deng said. "As long as it can catch mice, it's a good cat." Since then, China has done just that, pursuing a path of modernization that is ruthlessly pragmatic.

Deng Xiaoping's change of course for China presents a mental quandary. The Chinese government has the daunting task of finding congruence between being a Communist nation while actively pursuing modified market economic practices. To date, resolving this incongruity would seem to be elusive for the Chinese government. This unsettled situation has implications for urban Chinese identity. To reiterate the words of research participant Liu Rui: "We always feel unsafe, confused."

The Shanghainese are in search of a collective narrative that fully describes their past and their present while disclosing possibilities for the future. Ricoeur (1981:295) writes, "History... explores the field of 'imaginative' variations which surround the present and the real that we take for granted in everyday life. Such is the way in which history, precisely because it seeks to be objective, partakes of fiction." Ricoeur reminds us that historical events may be interpreted differently. Lawrence, with whom

I had an informal conversation in Shanghai, said that in most Chinese textbooks, perhaps only one or two pages are devoted to the Cultural Revolution. One or two pages could not possibly describe the complexity of events that took place within this ten-year period. Lawrence related that the information provided in school texts was vague and offered no specific details. Kearney (2002:155) asserts, "Storytelling…is never neutral." Kearney (2002:83) writes, "Narrative remembrance…is not always on the side of the angels. It can as easily lead to false consciousness and ideological dissimulation as to openness and tolerance." An ethical and comprehensive retelling of past events in urban China could fill the holes, the gaps of knowing "Who am I?" and also point toward "Who am I becoming?"

Imagination: Hopes and Dreams for the Future

In my research conversations, a theme that surfaced and resurfaced for the Shanghainese was the desire for expanded freedoms: the ability to access information, study or travel abroad, and give voice to new and different ideas that may or may not fall within the established paradigm of Communist thought. Eric said, "When you can't know everything that happened all around the world, you just feel like you are in jail." To cope with reality, or everydayness, people may imagine their world differently. Kearney (2002:25) writes that although the imaginary "is vicarious—i.e. unreal on the face of it—it is experience nonetheless; and one *more* real sometimes than that permitted in so-called reality." Kearney illumines an important concept: our unarticulated thoughts and our dreams also create our world. Shanghainese identity includes an historical past, a present-day reality, and an imagined future. In our thoughts, humankind is always free. When the only text available in Shanghai was Mao's "Little Red Book," one could still imagine reciting the poetry of Tang dynasty poet, Li Po (701 C.E. to 762 C.E.); or imagine reading the erudite commentary of Ding

Ling; or imagine enjoying a romance novel available prior to the Cultural Revolution.

The seemingly unstoppable trend of globalization would seem to have influenced the worldview of the Shanghainese. The Shanghainese hope for the ability to relocate and travel abroad freely, as China is now understood as belonging to a broader, global context. Eric said, "We think that American companies are good because we think it is more free in American companies. You can do what you want, what you imagine, in the daily life, and the company will give you the chance to make this the reality." Eric hopes to find employment where he can draw upon his own creativity. Gao Jin said, "I prefer to study abroad. I like Japan. I think the Japanese spirit is very high." Gao Jin's comment is echoed by many other Shanghainese. Young people seem to feel that there is a flat or dull quality to life in urban China, and they either hope to go abroad or to have greater diversity within their everyday lives. Zhong Mingyan's words were, "I have a lot of time, but I can only study, study, study." Chen Jingjing said, "After working, you just stay home. [There is] no free time to play." Inherent to our being-in-the-world is the desire to fully express both our individual and our collective identity.

Shanghainese identity is complex and multifaceted. Ricoeur (1992:116) hypothesizes that identity is composed of selfhood, *ipse*; sameness, *idem*; and the dialectic of the two. Ricoeur (1992:121) writes, "My character is me, myself, *ipse*." Ricoeur (1992:116) states, "The question of permanence in time is connected exclusively to *idem*-identity." *Idem*-identity is that which we recognize in another that is like our self. *Ipse* and *idem* are two expressions of identity that are one, for we are always in relationship with the other. Ricoeur (1992:121) writes, "To a large extent, in fact, the identity of a person or a community is made up of...identifications with values, norms, ideals, models, and heroes, *in* which the person or the community recognizes itself." In my research conversation with Eric and Nicholas, I said, "In Confucianism, the things that I know about, *xiao*, *li*, *ren* [filial piety; ritual; benevolence towards humanity] seem to reflect how people are in China, and these things are carried forward [into the present]." In my conversation with Li Shihai, I spoke of the 2008 Sichuan earthquake and the compassionate response by individuals and by the government: "I feel like the Shanghainese...and the government are making an effort to respond, and that there's deep caring." *Ren*, an expression of care for the other, quickly emerged in Shanghai following the Sichuan earthquake tragedy. Present-day Shanghainese identity holds a confluence of traditional China, global influences, past sufferings and past glories, largely unarticulated, and silent hopes for a better future. Words within the public forum may not necessarily acknowledge this mix of contemporary and traditional elements within society.

In Shanghai today, there would seem to be an absence of a collective narrative to tell the story of the Shanghainese. Claude Levi-Strauss (1978:20) writes, "Differences are extremely fecund." Shanghainese culture is unlike the culture of politically based Beijing or the anthropologically significant Xian. Shanghai reflects innovative entrepreneurship, creative and imaginative expression in the arts and in fashion, and the desire for greater freedoms in modern times. Ruth Benedict (1934:228) writes, "It is important to recognize that not all cultures are by any means...homogeneous structures." Benedict (1934:228) further states, "The danger of lopping off important facts that do not illustrate the main proposition is grave." Benedict raises an important issue: The history of the Cultural Revolution and other significant historical events would seem to be missing from the public forum of China today. Shanghai once excelled as a place of astonishing commercial development and artistic talent, was then silenced and oppressed during the Cultural Revolution, and then tenuously reclaimed a place in the post-Mao era, as noted by Hemelryk and Benewick, as the "City of Harmony" (2008:9). However, to arrive at harmony necessitates integration of disparate events within time. Kearney (2002:4) writes, "In our postmodern era of fragmentation and fracture... narrative provides us with one of our most viable forms of identity—individual and communal." A collective narrative that encompasses the historical past, present-day existence, and a projected future could be healing for the Shanghainese, whose official history is rife with gaps and aporias.

The articulated voices of the Shanghainese could likely fill the lacuna that renders incomplete Shanghai's history. The majority of the research participants of this study expressed the desire to have greater freedom of speech and praxis; there is more to be said and done toward this endeavor both by individual citizens and by governmental leaders in China.

Summary of Secondary Analysis

In my secondary analysis, additional and specific themes emerged through critical hermeneutic analysis: The Shanghainese strongly value stability, esteem moderation, and hope for greater freedoms within society. In reference to the educational philosophy of Paulo Freire, Father Denis Collins (2000:272) writes, "Authentic praxis is neither pure theory nor mere activism, but an ever re-created reality that provides an environment conducive to human growth away from oppression toward unfettered exercise of human freedom." Today, the Communist government of China has the opportunity to create congruence between word and action through praxis that is oriented toward the good life for all peoples within the lands we call China. Bernstein (1983:226) articulates, "The coming into being of a type of public life that can strengthen solidarity, public freedom, a willingness to talk and to listen, mutual debate, and a commitment to rational persuasion presupposes the incipient forms of such communal life." As Bernstein highlights, dialogue is essential to human freedom. The Shanghainese seek to be heard and to have a voice in public life. For this to occur, leaders in the Communist government would need to create a safe public space for dialogue to take place, and this would take time to mature due to past transgressions by figures of authority in history. By hearing the voices of its citizens, the government essentially opens up new possibilities for the future. Change is not always viewed as desirous by those in power; however, greater legitimacy for the government could arise from such action.

   Secondary analysis of the data also highlighted the theme of valuing moderation in Shanghainese culture. Research participant Liu Rui said, "I think Confucius's theory still works in modern China...Everyone is living in relationship with others." Liu Rui elaborated, "We just want to build good relationship with others. So, people care a lot about *ren, yi, li* [benevolence towards humanity, appropriate conduct, ritual]." Research participant Lu Ran said, "Even now, Chinese people are driven by... old, ancient principles." Lu Ran further said, "In Confucianism, people care about *xiao, li, zhong* [filial piety, ritual, loyalty]." Research participant Shen Lin spoke of preferring "our traditional thoughts." Participant Li Shihai spoke of the value of indirect speech as a manner of showing consideration for others. The Shanghainese appreciate the economic benefits of globalization; and, while they have indeed appropriated certain ideas and modes of being from the West, at the core of Shanghainese culture resides the practice of moderation in speech and in action. The Cultural Revolution would seem to be a period of time in China's history that moderation was not valued by those in power. Julia Kwong (1988:63) writes of the Cultural Revolution: "Any voice of moderation only invited criticism. Those who cautioned restraint could be criticized for being unfaithful to Mao's thoughts or, even worse, as counter-revolutionaries protecting the enemies." The aim of leadership during the Cultural Revolution was to eradicate existent cultural values and beliefs. Rodzinski (1988:126) writes of that time period that Red Guard units "put into effect the recommended struggle against 'The Four Olds' (ideas, culture, customs and habits)." A means of finding congruence between China's past and present would be for an authentic collective narrative to emerge, which includes the traumatic events of the Cultural Revolution.

Finally, secondary analysis of my research indicates that stability is paramount to the Shanghainese. Fareed Zakaria (2008:89) writes, "China has grown over 9 percent a year for almost thirty years, the fastest rate for a major economy in recorded history." Research participants Lu Ran and Liu Rui both spoke extensively of anxiety, tension and uncertainly in modern, urban China. Lu Ran stated that many people in Shanghai experience "stress, anxiety, depression." Lu Ran also said, "Rapid growth, rapid progress…it's not our proper speed." Liu Rui said, "I think the people who want more changes, the final goal is still to make the country become stable because now we are in fluctuation." The Chinese government could perhaps take greater steps to approach Shanghai's growth through well-thought-out policy and urban planning, and also provide increased social services to its people to better cope with rapid economic growth and the influences of globalization. Change reminds us of the value of stability.

In Chapter Seven, I provide a summary of my research findings on the subject of Shanghainese language, culture and identity. I further discuss the conclusions and implications of this study. Additionally, I present suggestions for further research.

CHAPTER SEVEN

SUMMARY AND CONCLUSION

Introduction

The teleological aim of this critical hermeneutic inquiry into language, culture and identity in Shanghai is to shed light upon present-day modes of being, past influences, and possibilities for the future for the people of urban China. The issue of identity is complex and multifaceted, for identity is not singular; rather, it has many expressions. Ricoeur describes identity as being comprised of *ipse*, selfhood; *idem*, sameness; and the constant, reciprocal relationship of self and other (1992:16). In Chapter Seven, I summarize the findings of my preliminary and secondary analysis, offer suggestions for further research in the areas of policy and curriculum development, and present my reflections and conclusion. Kearney (2002:155) writes, "There is no narrated action that does not involve some response of approval or disapproval relative to some scale of goodness or justice—though it is always up to us readers to choose for ourselves from the various value options proposed by the narrative." It is hoped that readers of this document will reflect deeply upon the lived experiences of the Shanghainese selected for this study, for theirs is a memorable story.

Summary of Research Findings

Introduction to Summary

This research is guided by critical hermeneutic analysis. The research categories of *mimesis* or temporality, appropriation, and imagination are employed to explore language, culture and identity in Shanghai. In my journal entry dated May 15, 2008, I recorded an informal conversation with landscape architecture student, Hong Yuqiu, who said, "I don't want an English name. I like to keep my Chinese identity." I would hear this sentiment many times during my research in Shanghai in May and June of 2008. The Shanghainese welcome the economic benefits of globalization, and have historically appropriated foreign dress and certain Western traditions; yet, at the core of Shanghainese identity resides the desire to adhere to traditional Chinese modes of being and doing.

Shanghai's present-day culture could be misinterpreted as merely following Western trends, but underneath this façade, one finds that Shanghainese identity is far more complex, integrating influences of Confucianism, Daoism, Buddhism, Communist thought, and globalization. Shanghai's culture holds an historic past of greatness and triumph, tragedy and suffering. The atmosphere of present-day Shanghai is tension filled, as it is understood that today's relatively prosperous times could suddenly give way to chaos and discord, in accordance with the Daoist pattern of "the sunny side" turning into "the shady side." As is the nature of time, an unknown future lies ahead for the Shanghainese, but their unique qualities of creativity, ingenuity and perseverance are reasons to hope for a brighter future for those who live in modern, urban China.

Preliminary Analysis

A preliminary analysis of the conversational text reveals themes of Aloneness and the Erosion of Trust; Survival, Materialism and Urban Alienation; Historicity and Shanghainese Identity; and Hope for a Better Future. The findings of these themes are discussed in this section.

1) Aloneness and the Erosion of Trust

The theme of Aloneness and the Erosion of Trust emerges from preliminary analysis of the data. Research participants Liu Rui, Lu Ran, Eric and Nicholas expressed thoughts that feelings of loneliness and mistrust are ubiquitous in modern, urban China. Research participants Chen Jingjing, Wang Xiaoyin, Gao Jin, and Zhong Mingyan each spoke of a preoccupation with earning money, indicating that the Shanghainese feel strongly compelled to compete and survive in contemporary Chinese society. The data indicate that there is a resultant distancing from others in society, although juxtaposed with this reality is the desire for greater relatedness with others. Research participant Lu Ran said, "It takes a lot of things to build up the trust, real friendship," suggesting that the word "friendship" in Chinese connotes a deep commitment and loyalty to another. Lu Ran explained, "Forgiveness is a very strong word in China," and being in relationship with another may require the conscious act of forgiving. Lu Ran's statements are a reminder that the Chinese language holds a particular worldview, grounded in historicity, yet simultaneously disclosing present and future understandings. Maturana and Varela (1987:212) write, "Because we have language, there is no limit to what we can describe, imagine, and relate. It thus permeates our whole ontogeny as individuals." The language of the Shanghainese reflects their values, traditions, and understanding of the world. In modern, urban China, the Confucian concepts *zhong*, *yi*, and *xiao* [loyalty, appropriate conduct, and filial piety] can still be heard, even though these words date back to the sixth century B.C.E.

2) Survival, Materialism and Urban Alienation

A second theme identified through preliminary analysis of the data is Survival, Materialism and Urban Alienation. In present-day Shanghai, one frequently hears the word *qian*, money, articulated in conversation; however, behind the pursuit of material wealth resides the less obvious desire for safety and well-being, in essence, survival. Today and historically in Shanghai's culture, there is a tacit understanding that money signifies a barrier between life and death. The concept of survival is integral to urban Chinese identity, as evidenced by the high rate of savings in urban areas. Fareed Zakaria (2008:92) writes, "China is...the world's largest holder of money. Its foreign-exchange reserves are $1.5 trillion, 50 percent more than those of the next country (Japan) and three times the holdings of the entire European Union."

The hard-working Shanghainese average ten-to-twelve-hour work days, leaving minimal room for fostering close relationships with others. In both formal and informal conversations, many Shanghainese spoke of loneliness and alienation in urban society. In the pre-Communist era, people often had nine or ten children, but the modern, urban family has been restricted by law to the one-child policy since February 1980 (Greenhalgh 2008:32). There are few loopholes for the urban population. Wealthy people sometimes pay a fine in order to have a second child, or go abroad to give birth, but for the vast majority of Shanghainese, the family is now comprised of father, mother, and a child without siblings. To reiterate the words of Hua Yun, "As one child, we are very lonely." An entire generation of urban youth has fewer familial relationships, and the frenetic work pace in Shanghai often occludes passing time casually with friends. As research participant Lu Ran expressed, "I am one child," and the young people of one-child families "don't communicate too much. They have been alone for a long time."

3) Historicity and Shanghainese Identity

Historicity and Shanghainese Identity constitute the third theme that arises from preliminary data analysis. In my research conversation with Liu Rui, I discussed the historical underpinnings of contemporary urban society. I said, "One of the things that I studied about China is that the dragon is the symbol of change and that throughout Chinese history there has been upheaval...With the Mandate of Heaven, the ruler only rules so long as he or she holds the Mandate." I further said, "There have been many changes throughout Chinese history. So, I think Chinese culture is a culture where people feel they must focus on survival and adapting to change." I noted that, concurrently, "there is very much a reverence for family and for society and...the Confucian belief of there being a connectedness to all people." I also spoke of Daoism, a contrasting thought to Confucianism, that also emerged in the sixth century B.C.E., a time when philosophical thought in China reached an apex. I said, "Dao is the way, following the path that opens up to you." In Daoist thought, if no path opens then no action is required. The influence of Daoist thought is, perhaps, not readily apparent in modernity; but, the data suggest that *wu wei* [nonaction] remains a remnant in Shanghainese thought. Research participant Nicholas reflected this mode of thinking when he spoke of change occurring gradually over time. Nicholas said, "Our government has China's best interest." On media access, Nicholas stated, "I think this situation is changing every day for the good. We can see more things."

The influences of globalization upon Shanghai's culture are quite evident: The city is fast paced, polylingual, high tech and high fashion. Research participant Li Shihai spoke of how life in Shanghai has changed since the onset of the Opening-Up period. Li Shihai said, "Decades ago...almost all of the people's time table is the same. So, get up earlier like six o'clock and start working maybe seven or eight, and stop working at four-thirty or five. Then, people had enough spare time to enjoy the evening." This prior, more relaxed lifestyle contrasts sharply with the hurried mode of the present, with work hours beginning early in the morning and ending well into the evening. The data suggest that the Shanghainese have indeed appropriated, and perhaps even intensified, Western business practices, and also embraced new and foreign technologies. However, this is but one facet of Shanghainese identity; the more remote past also influences the present. On May 19, 2008, I had an informal research conversation with a Shanghainese man, Wang Guanlong, who was wearing a beaded bracelet. Wang Guanlong shared that his mother, a Buddhist, had wanted him to wear the bracelet to keep him from harm and to bring about good luck. A declaration of faith, once banned during early Communism, may now be publicly expressed.

Absent from the public forum in Shanghai is any dialogue of the early period of Communism. In my informal conversation with He Xinyan, she avoided articulation of the words "Cultural Revolution." Instead, He Xinyan said, "It is difficult to find old things due to the 'ten-year period of difficulty.'" During the Cultural Revolution, art, music and books that were not viewed as aligned with Mao Zedong Thought were destroyed by Red Guards and fervent citizens. Perhaps some Shanghainese who previously felt oppressed in the pre-Mao era readily engaged in the destruction of that which was old, but most people acted out of fear—to not join in could constitute a death sentence. Citizens hoped to evade the label of "Anti-Revolutionary" and, silently, turned against their own moral compass. Gadamer (2004:69) writes, "When we speak of the 'nature' of things or the 'language' of things, these expressions share in common a polemical rejection of the violent arbitrariness in our dealing with things." Gadamer highlights that language is precise and intentional. In Shanghai today, thoughts of recent historical events, such as the Cultural Revolution or Tiananmen, remain hidden, unarticulated, rendering Shanghainese identity fragmented and incomplete.

4) Hope for a Better Future

Through preliminary data analysis, a final theme of Hope for a Better Future is identified. Research participants Chen Jingjing, Gao Jin, and Zhou Zijun spoke of material well-being as a hope for the future, emphasizing the need for safety and freedom from hardship. Others, such as Lu Ran, Liu Rui, and Eric, spoke of the desire for expanded individual and societal freedoms in urban China to become more fully whole in their ontology. Urban Chinese narratives point toward a desire for respect, justice, and being able to enjoin in the good life. Ricoeur (1992:197) writes, "The *just*, it seems to me, faces in two directions: toward the *good*, with respect to which it marks the extension of interpersonal relationships to institutions; and toward the *legal*, the judicial system conferring upon the law coherence and the right of constraint." A framework of possible action is defined within legalistic paradigms, and the law may aim for the fullest reasonable extension of human freedom or it may oppress human rights.

At present, the Shanghainese live within a world of limited choices and copious, restrictive legalities. The *hukou* system remains in place: One needs an official residency permit provided by the Chinese government in order to reside in a particular locality. Without such a permit, a person has no right to access housing, education or other societal benefits. The people of China cannot travel outside of the country without permission by the government. The Internet is monitored, so the Shanghainese and others must be watchful to avoid use of any banned words such as "democracy." Media is restricted to that which the Communist Party deems nonthreatening to its current hybrid disposition of being a Communist nation with modified market venues on the eastern seaboard. As citizens of the Communist state, the Shanghainese live under tremendous pressure to conform to predetermined rules of conduct. Fox Butterfield (1982:328) writes, "Constant exposure to public scrutiny and peer pressure makes life in China like living in an army barracks."

Secondary Analysis

Secondary analysis of the data identifies the themes of stability, moderation, and hope for greater freedom as being significant to the people of urban China. These themes were found to repeat within the data. In this section, each theme is explored as it relates to language, culture and identity in Shanghai.

1) Stability

The theme of valuing stability emerges as a recurring topic in formal and informal research conversations. Two research participants directly addressed the issue of stability in modern, urban China. In discussing economic development, research participant Liu Rui's words were, "The final goal is still to make the country be stable." Liu Rui communicated her hopes for more measured growth by the government in the future. Research participant Li Shihai said, "I prefer a little bit stable life." Li Shihai expressed concern that the job market in Shanghai is unpredictable, and therefore it is best to avoid taking risks whenever possible. He Xinyan, with whom I had an informal conversation, said that many people in China today still follow the ancient tradition of *feng shui*, a practice of arranging one's environment to be in harmony with nature and bring about good fortune. He Xinyan offered the examples of a white building paired with a black roof as being auspicious, and explained that corners of a tile roof in traditional style turn up toward heaven to honor the gods. The continuing practice of *feng shui* in modern, urban China is not mere superstition, but rather it suggests that there remains a reverence for the power of nature, and an understanding that quietude may accede to cataclysm.

On June 4, 2008, I wrote in my journal of the recent Sichuan earthquake tragedy, observing that the Shanghainese gave generously to the earthquake victims through donations of money and relief items, and through their good will towards those who suffer or who have lost loved ones. I wrote that the Shanghainese "seem to realize that the Sichuan earthquake victim could be one's mother, one's son, one's friend, one's colleague, or it could be me." Herda (1999:7) writes, "The identity of an individual is found in a moral relationship with others, which in aggregate form, makes up more than the sum of the membership." Further, Herda (1999:7) states, "When I change, the rest of the world changes." Individual identity is inexplicably bound up with the other, but identity is not lost to the other; rather, it comes toward a deeper fulfillment of our humanity. Ricoeur (1988:258) writes, "To think of history as one is to posit the equivalence between three ideas: one time, one humanity, and one history." The Shanghainese would seem to have an awareness that they are always in relationship with others through a shared ontology of existing and struggling in a fragile world.

Throughout China's history, there have been periods of natural disaster, political instability and change, and extreme suffering and deprivation. The older generation of China silently recollects past sufferings. The data suggest that, while urban youth do not have direct relationship with the past, they do have a vague understanding that present-day well-being could give way to less favorable times. Perhaps the faces, expressions, and silence of the older generation tell a story, for thoughts exist and may say something without words.

2) Moderation

The theme of acting in moderation is threaded within urban Chinese narratives. Shen Lin's words reflected this tenet when she said, "We choose the middle road." Gao Jin expressed, "Harmony is most important in China," suggesting that open confrontation and conflict are not the way of the Shanghainese. Li Shihai exhibited a belief in moderation when he said, "Everything can be negotiated and discussed." Fareed Zakaria (2008:113) states, "In talking to Chinese about their ways of thinking, one quickly recognizes that concepts like qi are as central to their mind-set as moral Creator...is to Westerners." Kathleen Higgins (2001:17) writes, "*Qi* is both spiritual and material," and "a person is a combination of light *qi* (the most refined and spiritual *qi*) and heavy *qi* (dispersed, more inanimate, and less powerful)." Higgins states that the development of light *qi* comes through spiritual cultivation (2007:17). However, there would seem to be less emphasis placed on spiritual cultivation in modern, urban China. Research participant Lu Ran said that today, "China is a country without any strong religion. So, most Chinese people now become atheist." It must be remembered that, during the ten-year Cultural Revolution from 1966 to 1976, open practice of religion was not allowed, which resulted in distancing young people from religious belief. Fareed Zakaria (2008:113) articulates that there is a "vacuum in Chinese spiritualism" in modern times.

The trauma of the Cultural Revolution continues to haunt Shanghai's present and future. Ricoeur (1967:6) writes, "An understanding of human reality as a whole operates through... myth by means of a reminiscence and an expectation." It is difficult to comprehend that, only one generation ago, the political and social environment of Shanghai was completely different, mired in zealotry and the eradication of culture, for the Cultural Revolution may be understood as an anticulture movement. The end of the Cultural Revolution was pivotal, for it brought back a tentative state of peace to the Shanghainese and others. The Communist Party has yet to initiate a public dialogue of the Cultural Revolution and other traumatic events from recent history, and this incomplete disclosure has resulted in fragmented identity and unanswered questions for the young people of urban China.

Globalization has brought change and perhaps another layer of uncertainty and confusion to the Shanghainese. The reappearance of foreign people and companies reintroduces different modes of being and acting in the world. Globalization confronts established cultural norms in Shanghai, but only the Shanghainese can decide that which they will take in as their own—appropriate—from that which was previously foreign. The data suggest that the Shanghainese hold mixed views as to the changed plane of living in a post-globalization society. Western economic principles, business models, and technology seem to be welcomed by the Shanghainese; however, the data suggest that core beliefs as to propriety and right conduct remain rooted in traditional Chinese modes of being. Clifford Geertz (1973:319) writes, "There is...no simple progression from 'traditional' to 'modern,' but a twisting, spasmodic, unmethodical movement which turns as often toward repossessing the emotions of the past as disowning them."

3) Hope for Greater Freedom

The final theme identified in secondary analysis is hope for greater freedom. Research participant Eric said, "I think what I need is freedom. I think when I live in this country, the government set up barriers from the outside world. But I can see improvement from the government. They are changing, but I need this happening right now." Eric's words suggest an exigency for the opening up of greater freedom. Research participant Liu Rui said, "People say in China women have a lot of freedom...but the truth is we don't have choice. Women, even though they want to stay home and be housewives, they can't." Liu Rui points out that, under current laws, work outside the home is obligatory for women. In my conversation with Nicholas, he communicated his belief that he could freely express ideas among his closest friends and family, but he exercised caution in written communication. Nicholas said, "We can say everything we want, but sometimes we just can't do it on the Internet because too many people will know that."

The Shanghainese and others in China do not possess rights to full freedom of speech. The Communist Party maintains the position that absolute freedom is not possible nor desirable. David Shambaugh (2008:44) cites the words of General Secretary Jiang Zemin when he spoke at a Chinese Communist Party Central Committee conference on June 13, 1989, shortly after the Tiananmen Square demonstration for democratic reform:

> The concepts of so-called democracy, freedom, and human rights spread by the Western bourgeoisie have aroused sympathy among some of the young intellectuals in our country. It can be counted as one of the ideological roots of the recent student unrest and turmoil. Many young students have some confused ideas in this respect…To them, "freedom" means they can do whatever they want. "Freedom of the press" was interpreted as meaning that one can express whatever views one wishes. How can that be possible? There is no absolute democracy or absolute freedom in any country.

Jiang Zemin assigns blame for the Tiananmen demonstration by Chinese youth to Western influences, but freedom is not merely a Western ideal, rather, it is a human ideal. The Communist Party today continues to largely reflect the stance of Jiang Zemin. Ricoeur (1981:83) writes, "Distortion is always related to the repressive action of an authority and therefore to violence. The key concept here is 'censorship.'" Ricoeur submits that truth is compromised when freedom of speech is restricted, and censorship is indeed a form of violence. Nicholas said, "I hope all the people around the world will know the real China, will know what's really going on here." There exists in modern, urban China a sincere desire to be known, to tell one's story, and to act freely within the constraint of consideration for the other. The Shanghainese imagine myriad possibilities for their future. Kearney (2002:81) asserts that one can "make the mistake of taking oneself literally, of assuming that one's inherited identity goes without saying." The narratives of Eric, Nicholas and other selected research participants suggest that the Shanghainese can imagine themselves inhabiting a different future that is not predetermined by what is or what has been. Kearney (2002:81) writes, "Each nation discovers that it is at heart an 'imagined community'...a narrative construction to be reinvented and reconstructed again and again." Current policies and practices of the Communist Party need not remain immutable. President Hu Jintao and other party officials have within their power the ability to move China toward a reconciliation of present-day contradictions, and open up a dialogue of past events such as the Great Leap Forward, the Cultural Revolution, and Tiananmen. These events happened, and to not speak of them does not signify that they never occurred. Kearney (2002:81) states, "Whenever a nation forgets its own narrative origins it becomes dangerous. Self-oblivion is the disease of a community that takes itself for granted...entitled to assert itself to the detriment of others." Initiation by Communist Party leaders of an open dialogue of past events could potentially be healing for the people of Shanghai, whose identity seems fragmented, incomplete.

Findings to Implications of the Data:

Policy and Curriculum

In this section, I discuss findings to implications of the data for potential governmental policy changes in urban China. In addition, I identify findings to implications of the data for curriculum development in the field of sinology.

107

Implications for Policy

The data suggest three critical areas for possible change in governmental policy in China. The findings identified include the following: 1) Expansion of personal and societal freedoms by the government, 2) Reconciliation of contradiction between China's formal policies and actions taken, and 3) Building a climate of trust within society through disclosure of past events and through open dialogue with citizens to discuss possibilities for the future.

1) Freedom in Praxis

The data suggest that the people of urban China seek expanded freedoms to speak, move about freely within China, travel to foreign nations, and have unfiltered access to information in the post-globalization world of present-day Shanghai.

2) Reconciliation of Contradictions

The findings of the data indicate that urban citizens hope for a reconciliation of contradictions, such as the stated adherence to a model of Communist ideology concurrent with practice of a modified market economy. Perhaps new language must emerge to accurately describe current political ideology. Another schism for urban Chinese identity is the absence of documentation on significant historical events, such as the Great Leap Forward, Cultural Revolution, and Tiananmen. Kearney (2002:31) writes, "History has an obligation to recount the past *as it actually was.*"

3) Building Trust in the Present

The findings of the data further suggest the need for the government to establish a climate of trust within urban society. The Communist Party has within its power the ability to rebuild trust through full disclosure of past historical events and open dialogue on human rights issues, thus moving toward a more egalitarian society in concert with written Communist doctrine. Joel Spring (2001:48) writes, "Clearly stated in the Constitution [of the People's Republic of China] are concepts of equality linked to social duties" and "professions of free speech limited by the requirement to speak out for morality and justice."

Implications for Curriculum Development

The findings to implications of this research for curriculum development in sinology are threefold. The data suggest the following: 1) Further studies of human rights issues in China, 2) Studies of the changed economic and thus political role of China in the global arena, and 3) Studies to address issues of belonging and identity in urban Chinese society.

1) Human Rights

An in-depth study of human rights issues in modern, urban China is suggested, exploring constitutional rights and legal reform in particular. Relative economic well-being alone does not satisfy the human spirit. The narratives of this research strongly suggest that people seek freedom in concert with rights established by international organizations, such as the United Nations, Human Rights Watch, and Amnesty International.

2) International Policy and Economy

The role of China on the global plane is changing, as China assumes a more potent role in world affairs. Fareed Zakaria (2008:88) writes, "China's awakening is reshaping the economic and political landscape." Post-globalization, urban China has surged ahead in economic growth, and Shanghai is recognized as a city fecund in innovation and entrepreneurship. The data suggest the development of curriculum to explore China's new role in international policy and economy.

3) Belonging and Identity in Urban Society

The development of coursework specifically on the issue of urban Chinese identity is suggested. The people of Shanghai are plagued by problems of urban alienation and extreme angst for economic well-being. The Communist government has limited each urban family to one child, unintentionally creating an entire generation of disaffected youth. The social welfare system of prior years has been replaced by market competition, and citizens are no longer entitled to universal healthcare or retirement benefits under current policy. The government's emphasis upon earning and furthering the national economy deter recognition of a fuller ontology, where deeper relatedness and, for some, a spiritual life would allow for a greater sense of belonging in urban society.

Future Research

I propose three recommendations for further research. The first recommendation for further research is to conduct a comparative analysis of urban identity and rural identity in China. The second recommendation for further research is to examine linguistic changes that reflect present-day Chinese identity. Finally, the third recommendation for additional research is to explore legal and governmental policy changes that influence human rights in China.

Conclusions

Present-day urban China appears modern and prosperous at a glance, yet beneath the veneer of prosperity reside historic truths, unarticulated but present nonetheless. Past sufferings of famine, violence, instability and fear remain embedded in Shanghainese identity. Deeply concerned for safety, stability and well-being, the Shanghainese appear to have a strong preoccupation with earning money; however, earning *yuan* actually signifies a barrier between life and death. Ricoeur (2004:66), citing Augustine, writes, "Great indeed is the power of memory." The Shanghainese cannot forget the atrocities of the Cultural Revolution, nor can they forget the historic deprivation of famine.

In addition to stability, the Shanghainese strongly value moderation. The Daoist principle of *wu wei* [nonaction] continues to influence the people of urban China, for they feel just in taking action only when a pathway unfolds and clearly points the way to be taken. Nonaction is often considered virtuous, and therefore leaders in China hold tremendous power to command the direction of the nation. The leadership of China today esteems economic development and increasing China's role in the global arena. The Chinese government views individual rights as subservient to the rights of government, which is, in theory, acting in the best interest of its citizens. However, this is not always the case, as exemplified by the forced relocation of hundreds of thousands of Chinese citizens in order to accommodate governmental urban development projects. But present-day modes of being have the potential to give way to new ways of being. Herda (1999:77) observes, "If we cannot imagine how our organization could improve, we can never live in a world different from the current conditions."

The people of Shanghai hope for justice and expanded freedoms, deeper trust and friendship in their lives, and meaningful relationship with others in the community. The Shanghainese typically express consideration for others in speech and action, as respect for others is a traditional mode of being in China that is not lost in the present. The Shanghainese demonstrate an orientation toward forgiveness of past tragedies and wish to move toward reconciliation and fulfillment in their lives today. The narratives of the selected research participants give voice to present-day realities of those in urban China. Richard Kearney (2002:14) writes, "Narrative matters. Whether as story or history or a mixture of both (for example testimony), the power of narrativity makes a crucial difference in our lives." Shanghainese identity holds tradition and change, that which is old and that which is new, and hopes and dreams for a better future.

Reflections

The people of Shanghai are talented, well-spoken and gracious in manner, and they also possess a sad quality. Urban identity seems fractured and incomplete, as there is no collective narrative in the public forum to hold together the disparate events of China's history. The Shanghainese search for congruence between Confucian tenets and recent globalization; between women's bound feet and present-day athleticism; between the zealotry and suffering of the Cultural Revolution and the relatively peaceful and prosperous times of the present. The Shanghainese are, as are all people, in search of truth, justice and freedom.

BIBLIOGRAPHY

Benedict, R.
  1934 Patterns of Culture. New York: Houghton Mifflin
       Company.

Bernstein, R.
  1983 Beyond Objectivism and Relativism: Science, Herme-
       neutics and Praxis. Philadelphia: University of Philadel-
       phia Press.

Browne, A.
  2005 China's Workers See Thin Protection in Insurance
       Plans. The Wall Street Journal, December 30.

  2005 Chinese Doctors Tell Patients: Pay Upfront, or No
       Treatment. The Wall Street Journal, December 5.

Buckman, R.
  2005 Why the Chinese Hate to Use Voice Mail. The Wall
       Street Journal, December 1.

Butterfield, F.
  1982 China Alive in the Bitter Sea. New York: Bantam
       Books.

Chen, N., C. Clark, S. Gottschang, and L. Jeffery, eds.
  2001 China Urban: Ethnographies of Contemporary Culture.
       Durham: Duke University Press.

Cheng, N.
  1986 Life and Death in Shanghai. New York: Grove Press.

Clayre, A.
1984 The Heart of the Dragon. Boston: Houghton Mifflin
Company.

Collins, D.
2000 Paulo Freire: An Educational Philosophy for Our Time.
Mexico City: Universidad La Salle.

Fairbank, J. and M. Goldman.
2006 China: A New History. Cambridge, MA: Harvard
University Press.

Fishman, T.
2006 The New Great Walls. China: Inside the Dragon.
National Geographic 213 (5): 130141.

Forbes, A.
2007 National Geographic Traveler: Shanghai. Washington,
D.C.: National Geographic.

Gadamer, H.-G.
2004 Philosophical Hermeneutics. Translated and edited
by D. E. Linge. Berkeley: University of California
Press.

2003 Truth and Method. Translation revised by J. Weinshe-
imer and D. G. Marshall. New York: Continuum Publishing Company.

Gaetano, A., and T. Jacka, eds.
2004 On the Move: Women in Rural-to-Urban Migration in
Contemporary China. New York: Columbia University
Press.

Gao, M.
2000 Mandarin Chinese: An Introduction. Oxford: Oxford
University Press.

Geertz, C.
1983 Local Knowledge. New York: Basic Books.

1973 The Interpretation of Cultures. New York: Basic Books.

Glain, S.
2006 A Tale of Two Chinas. Smithsonian, 37 (5).

Greenhalgh, S.
2008 Just One Child: Science and Policy in Deng's China.
Berkeley: University of California Press.

Hammond, K.
2004 From Yao to Mao: 5000 Years of Chinese History.
Chantilly, VA: The Teaching Company.

Harper, D., C. Pitts, and B. Mayhew.
2006 Shanghai City Guide. Melbourne: Lonely Planet Pub-
lications.

Heidegger, M.
1971 On the Way to Language. Translated by P. D. Hertz.
New York: Harper and Row.

1962 Being and Time. Translated by J. Macquarrie and E.
Robinson. New York: Harper and Row.

Hemelryk, S., and R. Benewick.
2008 Pocket China Atlas. Berkeley: University of California
Press.

2005 The State of China Atlas. Berkeley: University of
California Press.

Herda, E.
1999 Research Conversations and Narrative. Westport, CT:
Praeger.

Higgins, K.
  2001 World Philosophy. Chantilly, VA: The Teaching Com-
        pany.

Kearney, R.
  2004 On Paul Ricoeur: The Owl of Minerva. Burlington,
        VT: Ashgate Publishing Company.

  2002 On Stories. London: Routledge.

Kwong, J.
  1988 Cultural Revolution in China's Schools. Stanford:
        Hoover Institution Press.

Larmer, B.
  2008 Bitter Waters. China: Inside the Dragon. National
        Geographic 213 (5): 147169.

Levi-Strauss, C.
  1978 Myth and Meaning: Cracking the Code of Culture. To-
        ronto: University of Toronto Press.

Maturana, H., and F. Varela.
  1987 The Tree of Knowledge: The Biological Roots of Hu-
        man Understanding. Boston: Shambhala Publications.

Mencius
  2003 Dao De Jing. Translated and with commentary by R. T.
        Ames and D. L. Hall. New York: Ballantine Books.

Newman, R.
  2005 The China Challenge. U.S. News and World Report,
        June 20.

Ricoeur, P.
  2004 Memory, History, Forgetting. Translated by K. Blamey
        and D. Pellauer. Chicago: The University of Chicago
        Press.

1992 Oneself as Another. Translated by K. Blamey. Chicago: The University of Chicago Press.

1988 Time and Narrative, Vol. III. Translated by K. Blamey and D. Pellauer. Chicago: The University of Chicago Press.

1985 Time and Narrative, Vol. II. Translated by K. Blamey and D. Pellauer. Chicago: The University of Chicago Press.

1984 Time and Narrative, Vol. I. Translated by K. McLaughlin and D. Pellauer. Chicago: The University of Chicago Press.

1981 Hermeneutics and the Human Sciences. Edited and translated by J. B. Thompson. Cambridge, UK: The University of Cambridge.

1967 The Symbolism of Evil. Translated by E. Buchanan. Boston: Beacon Press.

Roberts, M.
2004 Dao De Jing: The Book of the Way. Translated and Commentary by M. Roberts. Berkeley: University of California Press.

Rodzinski, W.
1988 The People's Republic of China: A Concise Political History. New York: The Free Press.

Shambaugh, D.
2008 China's Communist Party: Atrophy and Adaptation. Berkeley: University of California Press.

Shaughnessy, E., ed.
2008 China: Empire and Civilization. Oxford: Oxford University Press.

Spring, J.
  2001 Globalization and Educational Rights: An Intercivilization
         Analysis. Mahwah, NJ: Lawrence Erlbaum Associates.

Thubron, C.
  1987 Behind the Wall: A Journey through China. London:
         Vintage.

Turner, V.
  1982 From Ritual to Theatre: The Human Seriousness of
         Play. New York: PAJ Publications.

Wang, P.
  2000 Aching for Beauty: Footbinding in China. New York:
         Anchor Books.

Yuan, B., and S. Church, eds.
  2000 Oxford Starter Chinese Dictionary. Oxford: Oxford
         University Press.

Zakaria, F.
  2008 The Post-American World. New York: W. W. Norton
         & Company.

APPENDICES

Appendix A: Letter of Invitation and Research Questions

Dear Mr./Ms.:

Thank you for agreeing to participate in an exploration of my dissertation topic. As you know, my research seeks to come toward an understanding of urban Chinese identity. I am inviting individuals to participate in this research and to share their ideas and reflections on the meaning of urban Chinese identity. It is anticipated that hearing the stories of people in urban China, and engaging in conversation, will shed light on the research topic. I hope to uncover a new understanding of urban Chinese identity, and, in this process, to create lasting relationship among each other and the research. I expect that the findings of this research may contribute to curriculum development in Asian studies, and also foster understanding between and among people of different cultures.

In addition to the opportunity to share ideas, I am asking your permission to record and transcribe our conversations. In doing so, our conversations will act as data for the analysis of the context I have described. Once transcribed, I will provide you with a copy of our conversational text so that you may review the same. You may add to or delete any section of the conversation at that time. When I have received your approval, I will draw upon our conversation to support my analysis. Data that you contribute, your name, and position will not be held confidential.

Below you will find a series of proposed questions. These questions are primarily for use as guidelines to direct our conversation. They also indicate my specific interest in the research topic. My hope is that the conversation provides an opportunity for us to learn something together through the exploration of the topic I have described.

Reflecting upon your life and your experiences, please consider the following questions:

1) What do you think is important to people in China today?
2) What are your thoughts on globalization and its influence on China?
3) Which aspects of modern Chinese life reflect the historic past? (i.e., Confucianism, Daoism, Buddhism, etc.).
4) What problems or tensions do you see in modern China?
5) What changes do you anticipate occurring in China in the near future?
6) What do you hope for your own future?

Again, thank you for your willingness to participate in this research. I look forward to meeting with you soon.

Sincerely,

Amy Pierovich

Researcher, Doctoral Student
University of San Francisco
School of Education
Organization and Leadership

Appendix B: Follow-Up Letter

Dear Mr./Ms.:

I would like to thank you once again for participating in conversation and contributing to my understanding of the research topic. Attached, please find a copy of the transcript of our conversation. Please notify me if you wish to add to or to delete any section of the conversation. I will make the changes you request and send you the revised transcript for your review. I sincerely appreciate your time and your contribution to this research.

Should you have any questions, please do not hesitate to contact me.

Sincerely,

Amy Pierovich

Researcher, Doctoral Student
University of San Francisco
School of Education
Organization and Leadership

Appendix C: Consent Form for

Research Participant

INFORMED CONSENT FORM
UNIVERSITY OF SAN FRANCISCO
CONSENT TO BE A RESEARCH SUBJECT

Purpose and Background

Amy Pierovich, a doctoral student in the School of Education at the University of San Francisco, is conducting a study on urban Chinese identity. The researcher endeavors to come toward an understanding of urban Chinese identity, and hopes that research findings will contribute to curriculum development in Asian studies and to better understanding between and among persons of different cultures.

I am being asked to participate in this research because I am a citizen of the People's Republic of China and I live in an urban area.

Procedures

If I agree to be a participant in this study, the following will happen:

1) I will complete a short questionnaire giving basic information about me, including my age, occupation, and contact information.
2) I will participate in a recorded research conversation about urban Chinese identity, with the understanding that I may add to or delete any part of the conversational text upon my review of the transcript.
3) I will give my consent for Ms. Pierovich to use the research conversation in her dissertation and in any publication.

Risks and/or Discomforts

1) It is possible that some of the questions on urban Chinese identity may make me feel uncomfortable, but I am free to decline to answer any questions I do not wish to answer or to stop participation at any time.
2) Participation in research is not confidential. The conversational text will be used in the dissertation and may be used in other published works.
3) The time required for my participation is approximately one-and-a-half hours; therefore, I may become tired or lose interest. I am free to stop the conversation at any time.

Benefits

There will be no direct benefit to me from participating in this study. The anticipated benefit of this research inquiry is to contribute toward an understanding of the research topic at hand.

Costs/Financial Considerations

There will be no financial cost to me as a result of taking part in this research.

Questions

I have spoken with Amy Pierovich about this research and have had my questions answered. Should I have further questions about the research project, I may contact Ms. Pierovich either by Internet xxx; or by phone xxx.

If I have any questions or comments about participation in this research, I understand that I should first contact the researcher. If, for some reason, I do not wish to do this, then I may contact the IRBPHS, which is concerned with protection of volunteers in research projects. I may reach the IRBPHS office by calling (415) 422-6091 and leaving a voicemail message, by e-mailing IRBPHS@usfca.edu, or by writing to the IRBPHS, Department of Psychology, University of San Francisco, 2130 Fulton Street; San Francisco, CA 94117-1080.

Consent

I have been given a copy of the "Research Subject's Bill of Rights" and I have been given a copy of this consent form to keep.

PARTICIPATION IN RESEARCH IS VOLUNTARY. I am free to decline to be in this research, or to withdraw from it at any point.

My signature below indicates that I agree to participate in this study.

_____

Subject's Signature   Date of Signature

_____

Signature of Person Obtaining Consent   Date of Signature

Appendix D: Pilot Study Transcript (2007)

Transcript of Conversation with Liu Rui

The conversation with Liu Rui took place on September 23, 2007, in Carmel, California. The research participant is a twenty-three-year-old graduate student at the University of San Francisco in Organizational Development. Liu Rui is from Lanzhou, Gansu Province, People's Republic of China. It may be noted that the Chinese surname is listed first, and then the given name. Ms. Liu selected the English name "Vivian" for herself. Thus, in the conversational text, I address Rui as Vivian.

The Conversation:

Amy Pierovich (AP): I am meeting with Vivian and we're going to talk about Chinese language, culture, and identity. And the first question that I want to pose to Vivian is what do you think about the quality of life in modern China?

Liu Rui (LR): It's a big question. I think it depends on what kind of people you are; I mean the status in society. If you are rich or you have a high prestige, of course, the quality of your life is good. Otherwise, it depends how poor you are. I know in some regions in the countryside, maybe 20 rmb [renminbi, China's official currency] is going to be enough for them to live a whole year. You won't believe this, but in Beijing maybe people just spend millions of rmb; sometimes it is even in dollars to buy a house, which they will never live in. So, the quality of life is, it varies from the status; if you are poor, the quality is bad; it is definitely bad. It is not like America. Maybe peasants [in America], they can live a better life than the citizens [of China]. Maybe they can still live a very cozy life; don't worry about money; don't worry about future; don't worry about living. But in China, if you are peasants, which means you are poor and everything is just bad, it's bad for you. So, I think this is very different from China and America.

AP: So, do you see a growing disparity, or difference between the people who have wealth and the people who don't have wealth?

LR: Yes, of course. And this gap is becoming deeper and deeper, of course.

AP: What do you think is important to people in China today?

LR: Important?

AP: What is important to them? For example, like people your age, people in their twenties and thirties. What is important to them? Are they thinking about job, family, making money? What are the things that are important to them?

LR: I think the most important thing is just making money, because life in China now is getting harder and harder. There are so many different reasons. I think one is the development of the country; I mean it developed too fast. So, when a country developed to this level, where the people are still in this level, I mean, both follow the thinking, the idea or quality of life at this level. But when we are trying to catch up with the development, it [the quality of life] goes this high. So, I think we are in the process of losing identity because we always feel unsafe, confused. The other reason is because of the policy. I don't know the word. The government forbid a family, I mean, a couple to have more than one kid. I don't know if you heard about this.

AP: Yes, the one-child policy.

LR: I am only child in my family, and so, by this way, we can control the population not growing too fast, but now the problems come out. I mean, for example, like me. I am an only child and if I married a boy who is also only child, which means two people, we have to support the whole family, I mean, four parents and maybe eight grandparents. And if we have a kid, just two people, we have to support the whole family, which is just impossible because life is hard. I think we cannot even survive by our own selves.

AP: Do you feel a lot of pressure?

LR: Yes, much. I mean, it's just impossible for me. I mean, if my parents don't work, they have no money. I can't support them really. This is really hard. So, what is the most important thing? Nothing but money because you don't have choice. You can say you have a very pure spirit or something; it doesn't work. Without money, you can't live.

AP: So, money is like safety then. You're looking at it from the perspective that money is like safety? And today in China, do you have social services to help older people and provide health care? What are those services like?

LR: I am just wanting to talk about this because we are trying to bring now more social service, but still it doesn't really work. I mean just too many people are retired. How can a government afford this? No, just very few people can benefit from this.

AP: So the benefits are limited.

LR: Just too many people and, you know, the service is very limited. What is more ridiculous is those people who can benefit from this service, they have already worked for years and they retired, and you know they are already living a good life, and now they just get benefit more. But for this, poor never ever; they remain poor and they can't change this situation because nothing could be changed. So, this is just really hard.

AP: Do you feel that for the older generation, there is a sense of so much rapid change and perhaps a sense of hopelessness? Have they lost hope because under Communist China, prior to the economic changes that have occurred in recent years, people had a safety net? I think that has changed, from what I understand. And so, I am wondering if, for the older people, it is particularly difficult because they feel like under Mao's China, they were safe in terms of having basic economic needs met and basic health care. That has changed from what I understand. For example, now in China, you pay for health care. Is that correct?

LR: Yes. I think so.

AP: So, how do you see the individual's obligations to family and to society? We just talked about this particular question a little bit. You were talking about for yourself, and, if you are married, that you have an obligation to your family to provide for parents and grandparents. You already addressed the question of family. How do you see the individual's obligations to society?

LR: Obligations?

AP: What is it that you feel that you should do for your country and for society as a person, as an individual person? Do you feel a sense of duty or obligation to China?

LR: I don't know how to say this, but I think most of people in my generation, we don't really have such sense of duty for the country because we don't really feel like we are eager to devote ourselves to this country because you can see that too many changes happened. And my generation are so spoiled. We are really [spoiled] because we are all the only child in our family; you can imagine how their parents would treat them. They give their child the best always and they devote themselves just to this kid. So, my generation, we don't care anything except for ourselves.

AP: That's a big change. I see that as a major shift from traditional China. I'm thinking of the Confucian tenets, *xiao*, filial piety, duty. I think that this quality is something that is carried forward. For example, it sounds to me like you still feel an obligation to parents and to your elders, to your family. But the shift that I see is that people no longer feel the obligation to society. That's what I see as the difference. Is that how you see it?

LR: I think it is true. Actually, I did a service, I mean, a research in my university, and the topic is just *xiao*, [and] how this *xiao* culture changed, I mean, from the historical Confucius will into modern society; how does it changed and which direction it goes. I think, I mean, our group did a research, I mean, the survey, among the student who are in universities. The result shows that we still have a feeling [that] we have the sense that we should feed back our families, my parents, something, but we are confused of how can we achieve this. See, I know and I want to support my parents. I want to have them live a better life, of course, because without them, there is no me. But I just don't know how I can afford this. So, we are all just confused. To the country, I think the people who are born in 1960s or 70s, they have more sense about duty, about devoting themselves to the country, because they are now maybe thirty or forty years old, so some of them are already successful or they gained what they wanted. So now the only problem is how can they feed back to the society. But for our generation, we are still too young to understand this. What's more is just the pressure that if you cannot live by yourself, [and] you cannot own your own life, how can you devote yourself to the society? No way, unless I am already successful, unless I don't need to worry about my life, my future, my parents, my kids. Otherwise, I don't have the time, I don't have the energy, I don't have the power to do this for other people, for other countries. No, just for the whole country, this is a problem.

AP: Do you see in Confucianism other things that are carried forward from the past, such as *yi*, appropriateness, *ren*, benevolence for humanity, *li*, ritual? Do you see any of these things carried forward in modern China that were practiced in the dynastic period? *Xiao*, I think, is still prevalent. But these other things, like ritual and appropriate behavior, do you now see any of these other qualities that are based on Confucian thought?

LR: Yes, sure, I think Confucius theory, it still works in modern China. Especially because of Confucius, I mean, the whole country, every people are living in relationship with others. Because without this relationship, then everybody, I mean, every single individual, it doesn't make any sense unless you have connection with others. And Confucius, he think that this is the most important thing in social life; that's why we always hide ourselves behind our words or performance in front of others. We just want to build good relationship with others. So, people care a lot about *ren*, *yi*, *li* just because we have to remain a good relationship. We have to behave ourselves to make a better performance. Actually, my paper this semester for Dr. Herda is going to talk about "face" because face in Chinese has two different meanings, and each different direction has very complicated meanings, and which is very interesting and also really important to our culture. We just pay too much attention to face, our appearance. To modern society, I think, this part it remains. But it [has] also changed some part. Because of the pressure, of course, we are more concentrated to wealth, to prestige. Because we care about this, so we care more about our performance in front of others to build up better relationship.

AP: I believe that Confucianism is still very strong in modern life and that this is a very big part of Chinese identity that is still carried forward. The other thing that I'm very interested in and want to know about is if you see any aspects of Buddhism. Is Buddhism still practiced in China, and also Daoism? Do you see aspects of Daoism in modern China? Do people follow these beliefs?

LR: I don't know much about Dao because it's too complicated; it's too mysterious. But I think that Dao is kind of the opposite of *ru*, which is Confucius. *Ru*, it encourages people to get into the world, to be more active, to be more aggressive. You have to devote yourself to the country. You have to build relationship with others. But, on the contrary, I think Dao, it says you have to behave yourself, you have to keep away from the world because it's bad, it's chaotic. And you just need to build your own world with yourself. So, you have to jump out, out of the world; don't get into it. So, I think that's why Dao nowadays is fading because it doesn't match the modern society. It's getting more interesting because, I think, now there's more Westerners; they started to learn something about both Confucius and Dao. Some of them, I think they prefer Dao better because getting into the world is really powering because the relationship with others is very complicated. But I think on the other hand, Dao, everything just follows by the rules of nature, so just let it be; don't try too hard to change something. You are the way you are. Just don't pretend. Don't cheat. I think that's [what the] Dao says. And about Buddhism, I don't know. I guess you already knew that Chinese, we don't have religion.

AP: Officially.

LR: We [don't have religion] just because Chinese people are very, you know, I shouldn't say, greedy, but we only turn to pray to the God, Buddhist or something, because we want something from this action. I mean, like I hope I can get a car, so I went to pray to the God; something like that. Otherwise, they never really pray or they never really appreciate God unless they want something. They want God to help them do something. I think it is very different from your Christian or other religions because you really believe in this God and you do whatever the God tells you to do. But we don't; we just want. It's not about God tell me to do something; I tell God please do something for me. So, I don't think this is real religion. So, nowadays, I think there are less people who really believes in Buddhism. But I think people in countryside, maybe some of them still have such religion because they can't do nothing to change their life except for pray to God.

AP: What I have studied about Chinese history is that there is a long history of famine, hardship, flood, natural disaster, and many other hardships. And also that only part of the land is arable. You can cultivate crops on some of the land, but that much of the rest it is not very hospitable. From what I know about Chinese history and the terrain is that there have been many hardships, and I see that in Chinese culture, survival has always been very important because of the harsh terrain. If the crop isn't good that year, people in an agricultural society have many hardships. I think that this is one of the reasons why there has been the focus on earning money, and that people think about survival more than in countries where crops are plentiful and food is plentiful. I think that's perhaps a difference if you compare the United States to China. I think that China has experienced hardship and upheaval, including political upheaval as well. So, there has been a lot of change and a lot of hardship, and people going through quite difficult times. I think that this changes the thinking of people to always have a consciousness about needing to have money and earning money so that you feel safe. I think that this is a part of Chinese identity, this need to survive and to be safe, and that this is very strong in Chinese thinking. Would you agree with that? How do you see it?

LR: Part of my final service in my university was a survey about peasants, their lives. You know now most of the researchers and the government, they think that the peasants are so eager to move out and to get into the cities and to find a job there and to get rid of their planting jobs there [in the country]. But I don't think that they are willing to do this. I mean, maybe they don't have any choice, because when I ask the peasants, actually they don't want to go out to work. They just want to stay home and do the planting because they are so enjoying this work. But they go out to work just for face. You can't believe this because everybody go out. If you don't go out which means you're inability or something, you don't have your ability to work, something like that. You can't earn money; you are loser. So, they don't want others to think that like this. So, although they don't want to, but they still go out to find a very hard job with very little pay just for face, maintaining their face in front of others.

AP: That's interesting.

LR: This region where I went is very close to Beijing, so they are not very poor. But in other countryside, I mean, some places extremely poor; they just don't have any choice, they have to go out. Because, in the cities, although you work hard, I mean, you are really tired, you are not safe, you have so many problems, but there is a chance that you can make money. But if you stay in the country, you will never earn money from that. I don't know. Our government are trying to help the peasants to gain more benefit from the planting, but it's just too many staffs and too much processes between the government and the individual, the peasant. Because, say, the government, the highest government, they give you a certain money to help yourself with your work or live a better life, something like that. They give a lot of money, but the second government, maybe the province, they took some for corruption, bureaucracy. And then it come to the city, and then it come to the town, and then to the village. Just too many different process, which, when the money comes to the peasant, it is very little even now. So, the policies, I think they are good, but it is just really hard to make it come true. So, no matter how hard the government are trying to help them, they still cannot be changed; the situation remains; they still poor, forever maybe.

AP: It's very hard for the peasants. In modern China, there are a lot of different influences from other countries, the whole movement of globalization. But I have the impression that that's affecting cities and urban areas more, and that, of course, the people in the countryside don't necessarily benefit from that because they are more geographically isolated. So, would you say that the cities are the ones that are benefiting more from globalization?

LR: Yes, that is for sure. Thanks to the Opening-Up, it makes a gap between the poor and the rich more and more wide, or deeper because like Deng, the leader who brought this Opening-Up…

AP: Deng Xiao Ping?

LR: Yes, Deng Xiao Ping. He encouraged some people. He saw that some of the people, they can become rich first, and then they can bring others to become rich. But the result is many people become rich suddenly, but they didn't help others to become rich as well. I talked to Dr. Herda yesterday about the several major changes happened in China in recent forty years. First one is Cultural Revolution in 1966, between 1966 to 1976, and, in this ten years, the whole country was just destroyed by ourselves. Chairman Mao, he forbidded people from going to school and from doing research work. So, actually, it is he who stopped our development. So, at that time, the whole values of the whole country, the culture, were totally changed. We didn't respect the people who are having knowledge, and opposite, if you used to be a slave of a land owner or if you are definitely poor or something like that, your status used to the lowest in the society; OK, you are safe , we respect you. But if you are professor, if you have relatives in overseas, or if you said something against Chairman Mao, you are dead meat. So, it's just we distort the whole culture. And, at that time, money is evil; it's Western stuff; we have to get rid of it. So, everybody was poor, as poor as hell. And everybody are the same. We are each single individual is exactly the same with others. People wear uniform, I think, during that time. There are maybe only three colors of clothing—gray, blue, and maybe black. So, all the women, they can't have long hair. So, people are actually just one because everybody is extremely the same, the [same] status [which is] no wealth. So, this ended in 1976, and two years later, Deng Xiao Ping, he brought the idea of Opening-Up, so from that day on, everything from a blank started to change. Because of this, we are starting from zero, so it's easy for some people to get rich or successful in very short time, but other people who did not grasp the opportunity to get rich, they still remain poor. So, from then on, the gap, it generate.

AP: So, where do you think China is going now? Where do you see China going in the next five or ten years? What are the trends or what is the direction do you think China is going?

LR: I don't know. But I don't feel confident about that because, you know, from 1980s, the society has changed a lot. In the Cultural Revolution, we think money is the least important thing. But, after the Opening-Up, nothing [else] is important, only money; only making money is only important thing. And, nowadays, we hate the rich people; we think they are cheaters. They are liars because they get rich too fast and they don't care about others. But, also, we hate the poor because they don't have ability to live a better life, so we have discrimination on that. But they still becoming eager, so I don't know the direction of the whole country, which [way] it will go. Actually, nowadays, the leaders are upholding that we have to be honest to others. We have to rebuild a new system which is rely on the trust or sincere. But it's really hard because, say, OK, I can be honest to others, I won't cheat in my business, but how can I prevent myself from others cheating me? It's really hard. So, if I can't stop them to lie to me, why should I stop? So, we already did this for twenty years. It's really hard to change this situation. I think in March of this year, the new chairman, Hu Jin Tao, he said some words. I don't know the English, but it's sixteen very simple sentences. Eight of them is what you should do, like you have to be good to others or you have to be sincere or be honest, and don't think that money is the most important thing; something like that.

AP: To try to create some balance in society? Because it seems like it's changed from during the Cultural Revolution, like you were saying, that money was seen as actually evil and now money is highly valued. It sounds like in modern China, people are trying to come towards a sense of perhaps moderation, of also looking at other aspects that may be important, and not simply money. Is this the concept that Hu is introducing? To bring some balance back into society? It seems like the modern era, from Mao and the beginning of Communist China to the present day, has been a time of lots of changes, and I think it's very difficult for people to go through so many changes. And yet, I think that within Chinese culture there are certain core beliefs that carry people forward through change. One of the things that I studied about China is that the dragon is the symbol of change and that throughout Chinese history there has been upheaval. This has occurred throughout Chinese history and, of course, with the Mandate of Heaven, the ruler only rules so long as he or she has the mandate, or the right to rule because he or she is acting in the right manner. So, if you lose the Mandate of Heaven and the gods are no longer with you, it is because you didn't act correctly. With so many changes and upheavals throughout Chinese history, I think it is a culture where people feel that they must focus on survival and adapting to change or trying to. Still, at the same time, there is very much a reverence for family and for society, and what you were talking about—the Confucian belief that there is a connectedness to all. Daoism was a contrasting thought at the time of Confucianism, with the Dao being the "way," being more open, and following the way that opens up to you, whereas Confucianism has more structure. What do you think is unique about Chinese identity? What do you think is unique about the way Chinese people see themselves and also see themselves in the world? What do you think is unique? What is particularly Chinese? Not German, not American, not Japanese. What do you think is unique to Chinese identity?

LR: For me, I would say "face" because, it's too hard to say, actually have two different backs of face: one is *lien*, the other is *mienzi*. *Lien* is what you gained the day you were born, so this is your character. If you do something wrong, you do something bad, which can cause losing face; this losing face is losing your *lien*, because that is a shame, that is bad; you are a bad person. But *mienzi*, that is the surface of your face, so that refers to the status, the prestige, the wealth, something like that. So, you can gain *mienzi* or you can lose *mienzi*.

AP: So you have innate qualities with which you're born, but then, with *mienzi*, you can build up your character and your success and your status through your actions.

LR: Yes, through your actions in front of others. And this gaining *mienzi* and losing *mienzi* is related to your action for your relationship with others because this *mienzi* is gained by others. So, for me, I think it is like where Ricoeur says *ipse* and *idem*. I think the *lien* is kind of like *idem*, which cannot be changed. Sometimes you can lose your *lien*, which is because you did something very bad. Otherwise, you won't lose it. But for *mienzi*, it is like *ipse*; it is always changing. So, a very typical example is the gift. Chinese people like to give gift to others, especially when the festival, very traditional festival, say, like Mid-Autumn Day. When that day comes, it's very important festival; we eat moon cakes, and we give moon cakes as gift to others. So, usually, this moon cake is very cheap, is very affordable, but for some rich people or high status people, they want to give such gift which is very luxury, maybe one hundred times of the regular price. And they give such fancy gift to another person who has a same or even higher status than him. And through this action, both of them, the receiver and the giver, they both can gain *mienzi* because they both deserve this such fancy, luxury gift. Otherwise, if this guy gives another people a very cheap [gift] or something doesn't match his status, both of them will lose their *mienzi*, because this guy will think that the giver doesn't respect him; he is not sincere to him. But the giver will think that the receiver, he doesn't deserve a better gift. This action will cause both of them lose their face. But I think in Western cultures, this is not important; a gift is just a gift. If you put your heart into it, it doesn't matter how much it is; something like that. But in China, the price of your gift is very important.

AP: That's fascinating, Vivian. So a big part of identity for Chinese people, then, would be honor because it illustrates the respect inherent in relationship with others. I am hearing from what you have been saying that there's very much a sense of the individual being in relationship to others and that this is very important. And that the idea of saving face, which is not particularly prevalent here in the United States, in China, is extremely important—showing honor, saving face, treating others with respect, and expressing your own character. In *Oneself as Another*, Paul Ricoeur writes a lot about character, and these qualities of character are all very important, if not critical, to the Chinese identity. And what do you hope for your own future?

LR: My own future; I'm not so sure. Actually, before I came here, I was thinking that once I finish my program here I will go home as soon as I can and find a job there or something like that. But, after I came here, when you really compare the difference between the two countries, now I think maybe I will live here. I mean I will try to stay here because you can't imagine; I will try to stay here because earning a life in China is really hard. It's not only about your ability, your knowledge, such stuff; you have too much things to be considered, like your relationship with others. I don't have a very good connection with the people who can help me to get a good job or something. Because in China, if you don't have such connection, it will be very hard for me to get a very good job.

AP: Are you referring to *guanxi*, connection? Which is a different way of thinking than here in the United States, isn't it?

LR: Yes, but in China, it is very important because, no matter the quality of the employees, if someone has a strong connection with *guanxi*, very good; then they just [get] hire. So, it's really hard. And within this company, you are a secretary, and another guy has the same position as you, but he has a better connection with the boss, so he can [get] promote, but you cannot. It doesn't matter, your ability.

AP: So, your *jihui*, your opportunity, is limited when you have to go through connections to get ahead, instead of it being based on your ability, your skill, your motivation. So, it's difficult. Since that's still in practiced in China, do you feel like you would have more opportunity here?

LR: Maybe. I'm not sure because anyways I am just a foreigner here. I also have many limited for myself. Still, I think the relationship here is very simple. If you work hard, or if you are eligible, you still have a lot of chance to work at a better place. You can earn your life by yourself. But in China, that is impossible because everybody lives in connection, in relationship with others. If you don't, you cannot survive. But on the other hand, it is very difficult for you to be in a good relationship with people who have a higher status or people who can help you with this stuff. I think I am so tired of that. I don't want such a complex life. I don't want to cheat. I don't want to lie. I hate this. It's just too tiring. The policies in China, I think you don't have many freedoms to do whatever you want. What do you say? What do you do? You're just under the control of the government, the leaders. And sometimes even if the law, it doesn't says you can't do this, but we have a very strict moral rule: Everybody are watching you. So, anyways, you can't do this; this is ridiculous to them, so you just won't be able to do. I think maybe I should just stay here. I really like the life here; it's very simple. Maybe it's not easy; it's hard, but it's simple. I just like this way.

AP: I'm very fascinated by the Chinese language because you have many meanings within one character. You write the character and then within the character you have perhaps several meanings based on the root of the character, and then additional brush strokes adding more meanings to the character. And now of course Pinyin is the Romanization so that people can pronounce the words. I find that the Chinese language is fascinating. What do you think is unique about the Chinese language? What I see is that there are multiple meanings. A spoken word can have many meanings. There are many homophones, words like *ma, ma, ma, ma*, with the varied tones. So, you can have one word; just hearing it, you can have many different meanings. But also the characters themselves are very rich. I am trying to think of an example. I believe the word "harmony" is a woman under a roof.

LR: I don't know the word. Is that this character? Woman under a roof. This one?

AP: Yes.

LR: It means "safety" or "peace."

AP: So, you have two meanings within a character. You have the meaning of this stroke, you have the meaning of the other part, and then you have the meaning as a whole. What do you think is unique about the Chinese language and how does that relate to a Chinese identity? How do you think that is different perhaps from someone who is English speaking or speaks a language that isn't based on characters?

LR: I think Chinese language is very creative in the sense to our ancestors. They created such characters. It's like a picture; everybody knows it. Like this character is a very ancient style, maybe thousands of years. What do you think of this?

AP: Water?

LR: Yes, exactly. So each character conveys a picture of stuff; maybe of action or maybe just of a thing. Like English words, you also have to find the roots in words. The structures also contain roots, and some of the roots serve the pronunciation. Once you see this character, once you see the part and other roots, [they] convey the meaning of the character. Sometimes they work together; sometimes they work apart. I think this is related to our traditional culture, like this one you just said. It means not only a roof, but it also means a room or a house. So, a woman in a room or a house, it means "peace"; it is a family. When you see a woman sitting in a room, you just see a picture of peace, of harmony.

AP: So how do you say that in Chinese, this particular character in Chinese?

LR: *An.*

AP: I think the Chinese language is so fascinating because you have so many symbols within the language. And when you translate from Chinese into another language, for example, into English, very often something is lost in the translation, I feel. Because, for the Chinese speaker, you're reading it and you understand the word "peace." Within the word "peace," there are many different submeanings, underlying meanings. And so, to me, this makes the language extremely rich and Chinese thought very complex, operating on a very high level. Sometimes, when I listen to a translation from Chinese into English, for example the names of the countries, like *Zhong Guo*, Middle Kingdom, Middle Nation, I realize the origin of this goes back to the Chinese people believing that they're at the center of the world. But somebody that hears the word "China" simply thinks that that means China. They don't understand the more complex meaning of *Zhong Guo* or *Mei Guo*, for example, Beautiful Nation; this is thought of as a beautiful place, that it has that perception, or *Jia Na Da*, Canada. So, each country has a particular meaning that is not conveyed in the translation when you just translate into English. I think that this is a very interesting thing about China and Chinese identity because the identity includes this language which is so very rich. Although, in Chinese history, I believe approximately eighty-five percent of the people were illiterate up until the time that Mao Zedong assumed power and commenced Communist rule. So many people were illiterate and, little by little, more and more people have become literate. It is my understanding that more people read today at least on a basic level. The Chinese language is so rich and interesting; this is one of the things I want to look into further. The other question I wanted to talk to you about is what problems or tensions do you see in modern China? Do you see people wanting even more change? Are they feeling like there is too much change? I know, for example, that certain words are banned in China. I know that there are some people who would like to have greater freedoms, such as freedom of speech, freedom of, as you were speaking about, moving around, and having greater freedom to travel or to go to a different location. Do you think that people are now seeking more change or more stability? Where do the tensions lie in Chinese culture at this time?

LR: I think it is hard to say. For some people, they call for more changes, and for others, they hope it can be more stable. But I think the people who want more changes, the final goal is still make the country be stable because...now we are in fluctuation. Some is good; you don't need to keep balance. But some, you really have to make a equilibrium between the changes. So, I hope, and many people hope that we can be more free to move around the whole country or even move to other countries. We also hope life could be easier. We want to work hard, but most of the time it doesn't mean [if] you work hard, you can gain more. So, we just hope that it will be more equal in the society because some people, they don't work but they earn a lot. They have everything. But some people, they work a lot, they work so hard but they get nothing. We just want this society to be more equal.

AP: And to bring more balance may be a direction for China because there has been a lot of rapid growth. Perhaps more balance and stability can be brought to the current situation?

LR: Because the country, it developed too fast without waiting for the people to get [to] adapt to it. So now, we have so many people who can't find a job, so many people who can't go to hospitals; just too many problems. And the country is still developing without paying attention to such problems. Although the leaders may know there are such problems and they want to begin to change it, but it's just you have too much to do; you can't concentrate to just one aspect. So it's really hard.

AP: It's very overwhelming, isn't it? Because of such a large population, and to provide services to everyone is extremely challenging. It's really very difficult.

LR: Yes, it's something like medical, education, safety; too many problems. You can't solve more than one.

AP: And when there's this trend of people moving from the countryside into the cities, you have a migratory population and some of those people in the cities don't have rights to education or the permit to actually live and work there. It seems like that creates a certain tension within society because you have some people who have the right and some people who don't. And then people coming from perhaps different regions may have different customs and practices. And there is a big difference in the level of education from the people in the countryside and the people in urban areas. Because there is probably a lot more opportunity for schooling and education, say, if you're from Shanghai or Beijing than if you're from a rural area, even outside of Kunming, or some of the more remote areas. There is definitely more opportunity in the cities now, and it's going to be interesting to see where things go politically and economically from this point. I think that we both touched on the need for more stability within such rapid change. It seems like it creates a high level of stress for people in their lives and that life is difficult. And there's a lot of pressure, especially on your generation, the younger generation, that is tremendous because there's got to be a lot of expectation from the parents since they have only that one child. So, there's a huge expectation for that one child to provide financially for the family and to carry on the family name, I suppose, if it's a male. But if it's a female child, it's not the tradition to carry on the family name. Is that correct?

LR: Yes.

AP: And in the dynastic period, it was the male child who supported the parents, but today, now with the one-child policy, the daughter is also expected to provide for the parents. Is that true?

LR: Yes, because you don't have choice like me. I am an only child. No matter I am a boy or girl, I have to support my families. People say Chinese women have a lot of freedom; they are equal with men because they go to work; they are not housewives. But the truth is, we don't have choice. Many women, even though they want to stay home and be housewives, they can't. If you don't go out for work, for job, your husband can't support a whole family. You don't have choice, that's why you have to go to work.

AP: So it's an economic reality that both people must work. And do you think you will continue on for the doctoral program after you finish the master's?

LR: No, I don't think so. Because in Chinese culture, there is an idiom: There are three kinds of human in the world; one is man, one is woman, and one is woman doctor, just a woman who has a doctor degree. That is a third kind of human in the world because in China, in marriage, the man is supposed to get married with a woman whose status is lower than him. So, if you are a woman doctor, what kind of man you can find? Too limited.

AP: I see. So, you would like to finish your master's degree and perhaps not get the doctorate because you want to have a marriage.

LR: Yes.

AP: Vivian, I would like to thank you for participating in this interview with me. Your contribution to this research is much appreciated and I have enjoyed talking with you. I wish you the best in your life.

LR: Thank you very much for having me participate in your research. I enjoy talking with you too.

www.ingramcontent.com/pod-product-compliance
Lightning Source LLC
Chambersburg PA
CBHW070922270326
41927CB00011B/2677